BARBARIANS
IN THE SADDLE

BARBARIANS IN THE SADDLE

An Intellectual Biography of
RICHARD M. WEAVER

JOSEPH SCOTCHIE

TRANSACTION PUBLISHERS
New Brunswick (U.S.A.) and London (U.K.)

Library of Congress Catalog Number: 97–16718
ISBN: 1–56000–321–9
Printed in the United States of America

Library of Congress Cataloging-in-Publication Data

Scotchie, Joseph, 1956–
    Barbarians in the saddle : an intellectual biography of Richard M. Weaver / Joseph Scotchie.
        p.   cm.
    Includes bibliographical references and index.
    ISBN 1–56000–321–9 (alk. paper)
    1. Weaver, Richard M., 1910–1963. 2. Politics and literature—
United States—History—20th century. 3. Conservatism—United
States—History—20th century. 4. United States—Intellectual
life—20th century. 5. Criticism—United States—History—20th
century. 6. Civilization, Modern—20th century. 7. Southern
States—Civilization. 8. Civilization, Western. 9. Rhetoric—
Philosophy. I. Title
PS29.W43S36   1997
814'.54—dc21   97–16718
                                                                          CIP

Contents

Acknowledgments

Thanks to Polly Weaver Beaton, sister of Richard Weaver and Josephine Osborne, cousin of Richard Weaver for biographical information. Thanks also to Professor Ted J. Smith III and Mr. Louis Dehmlow for other insights into Weaver's life and career. Much of the bibliography was gleaned from an earlier work prepared by Paul Varnell from the 1968 Arlington House edition of *The Southern Tradition at Bay* (now out of print). The Special Collections section of the Jean and Alexander Heard Library at Vanderbilt University, Nashville, Tenn. has the most extensive collection of Weaver papers and letters. Michael Sims, an employee at that library provided information for the chronology. Most of all, thanks to my wife Anna for the research, proofreading, and for believing in this project when the author held far less confidence in it.

Richard Malcolm Weaver Chronology

March 3, 1910. Born in Asheville, N.C. Lived in Weaverville, North Carolina.

1916. Family moved to Lexington, Kentucky.

1927–1932. Attended University of Kentucky. Member of Phi Beta Kappa. Received A.B. degree.

1933–1936. Attended Vanderbilt University. Was a teaching fellow. Received masters in English.

1936–1937. Instructor in English at Alabama Polytechnic Institute.

1937–1940. Acting assistant professor at Texas A & M.

1940–1943. Student at Louisiana State University where he worked with Cleanth Brooks and Robert Penn Warren. Summer sessions at the Sorbonne, Harvard University, and the University of Virginia.

1943. Received Ph.d from Louisiana State University.

1944–1963. Professor of English at the University of Chicago.

1948. *Ideas Have Consequences.*

1949. Won University of Chicago Quantrell Award for excellence in undergraduate teaching.

1953. *The Ethics of Rhetoric.*

1955. Russell Kirk establishes *Modern Age*. Weaver writes the inaguaral number's first essay, "Life without Prejudice."

1957. *Composition: A Course in Writing and Rhetoric.*

1958. Participant in Vanderbilt University Literary Symposium.

1962. Recieved Young Americans for Freedom Award at a rally in New York's Madison Square Garden. Inscription reads for "service to education and the philosophy of a free society."

April 9, 1963. Died in Chicago, Illinois.

1964. *Visions of Order.* Richard M. Weaver Fellowships established by Intercollegiate Studies Institute.

1965. *Life Without Prejudice and Other Essays.*

1968. *The Southern Tradition at Bay.*

1970. *Language is Sermonic.*

1983. The Rockford Institute, Rockford, Ill., establishes the annual Richard M. Weaver Award for Scholarly Letters.

1985. *The Ethics of Rhetoric* reissued by Hermagoras Press.

1987. *The Southern Essays of Richard M. Weaver.*

1989. *The Southern Tradition at Bay* reissued by Regnery/Gateway.

1995. *Visions of Order* reissued by Intercollegiate Studies Institute.

Introduction: A Man Out of Step

The purpose of this book is to introduce the reader to the works of Richard M. Weaver. Our subject is associated with two well-known twentieth-century intellectual developments, the Southern Agrarian literary movement and the post-World War II conservative reaction to the statism of the New Deal. The former came into being primarily through the 1930 publication of famous Agrarian manifesto, *I'll Take My Stand*. Weaver studied at Vanderbilt under John Crowe Ransom in the early 1930s, when Agrarianism was still a promising force. Although his stay at Vanderbilt did not fully bring him around to agrarianism, he was committed to traditionalism by the early 1940s, when he wrote his Ph.D thesis (later published as *The Southern Tradition At Bay*) at Louisiana State University under the direction of Cleanth Brooks. A string of cogent and well-argued essays about Southern culture and literature in the 1950s gave Weaver his well-earned identification with the Agrarians.

While Weaver was a leading disciple of the Agrarians, he was also an important philosopher of the postwar conservative intellectual movement. That spirited opposition to the triumph of statism in American and Europe was launched in part by Weaver's 1948 book, *Ideas Have Consequences*. Historians identify Weaver, along with Austrain economists Friedrich A. Hayek and Ludwig Von Mises, Russell Kirk, Whittaker Chambers, and James Burnham as the intellectual founders of a movement that had three main focuses: The libertarian economist wing (Hayek and Von Mises), a strong anticommunist ideology (Chambers and Burnham), and the traditionalist wing. Weaver, along with

Kirk, is widely recognized as the founder of the traditionalist element of modern conservatism—a philosophy concerned with preserving ancient Western traditions and pieties amidst the enormous changes and pressures brought on modern society by the forces of technology, industrialism, and the rapid urbanization of the hithero agrarian American republic.[1]

Weaver remains a revered figure to the remnants of the Old Right. In the 1960s, the Intercollegiate Studies Institute established fellowship awards in Weaver's name to students interested in pursuing graduate studies. And in 1983, the Rockford Institute accorded Weaver its highest honor, establishing, in his name, the annual Ingersoll award for scholarly letters. The institute also confers the T.S. Eliot Award for Creative Writing. By being elevated to the same level as one of the century's most famous and revered literary figures, Weaver was finally given proper recognition as an important thinker in his own right. Winners of the Richard M. Weaver Award for Scholarly Letters have included Kirk, Andrew Lytle, Robert Nisbet, John Lukacs, Edward Shils, Forrest MacDonald, and Eugene Genovese.

A scholar could find several themes to Weaver's work; this study will concentrate on his view of man and society. An honest view of man and the quest for civilized communities are themes that appear consistently throughout Weaver's work. To Richard Weaver, one of the great tragedies of modernism was its perverse—and dangerous—view of man. Whereas philosophers and poets throughout the ages viewed man as "a creature somewhat below angels" who was engaged "in a monumental struggle for his soul," twentieth-century man was considered a "naturally good" being who could be perfected by social engineering. Worse yet, modern man, in the age of megalopolis, has lost his "manuevering room," his chance to develop his individuality or personality. He has disappeared into the masses, disintegrating into an "economic unit" and a "consuming animal," seemingly incapable of committing heroic acts that defined other epochs of Western history.

Richard Weaver had sympathy for existentalist thought that surfaced in the 1940s and 1950s. He praised novelists such as Ernest Hemingway whose heroes rebelled against massness and conformity. But existentalism was not enough. In his autobiographical essay "Up From Liberalism," Weaver wrote that "a man saves himself *if* at all, by bringing his community around to right reason." Man must not be a selfish being, concerned only with his own welfare. He is born into a living community and must give some of his life to its well-being. There are higher ideals than individual fulfillment. Weaver would prefer nations (especially his own United States) to be made up of citizens living with somber republican responsibilties rather than as ravenous and indulgent consumers. The phenomenon of modern decadence—and the possibility of its permanance—was never far from the author's mind.[2]

What constitutes a civilized society? Weaver was concerned above all, with the health of established cultures; since such cultures are phenomena that order civilized societies. In his finest statement on the subject, "The Importance of Cultural Freedom," Weaver boldly states that cultures must remain exclusive; they must reject outside forces or ideas that would destroy them. Several elements define culture: geography, climate, religion, race, liturgy, poetry, epics, and mythology. From a well-defined culture spring forth laws that members of a society consent to live by. In other words, order isn't *imposed* upon them, it is something defined by the culture they are comfortable living in.

Order itself was an important theme in Weaver's work. His last book (although not his last planned book) was entitled *Visions Of Order*. But Weaver lived in an age when merely the term "order" carried negative baggage and was usually savaged as a repressive idea. Even to this day, Weaver is criticized as an absolutist whose views on order, if ever practiced, would lead to a theocracy threatening individual liberty. In his 1992 book, *The Conservative Crackup*, columnist R. Emmett Tyrrell, Jr. complained that for decades "liberals were habitually condemning opponents on their right as authoritarians, usually with no more justification than was provided by the writing of Weaver." Tyrrell then seems to agree with Weaver's liberal foes, adding that the philosopher's "idealized world of moral absolutes, if unleavened by tolerance, might indeed lead to authoritarianism...[T]o be sure, Weaver's theocrat is potentially a threat to human freedom, but so is the president of Stanford University." Tyrrell reads Weaver as extolling "immutable principle, hierarchy, and restraint" and directing readers to "important things, the nature of man, the quality of men's souls." But nowhere in his short brief against Weaver (he also complains that Weaver's conservatism does not move readers to "enthusiastic, backslapping political action"), does Tyrrell present examples from Weaver's work that might be seen as posing a threat to human freedom, nor do we know where Weaver's dreaded theocrat comes from.[3]

Richard Weaver's body of work was based on an exhaustive study of Western philosophy, history, and literature. He certainly was one of the most well-educated intellectuals of his era, a Phi Beta Kappa at the University of Kentucky, an M.A. at Vanderbilt University, a Ph.D from Louisiana State University, with summer studies at Harvard University, the University of Virginia, and the Sorbonne in Paris. His study of the West led him to favor Plato's vision of the "beautiful and good" as articulated in the *Phaedrus*; the feudal order of the Middle Ages and the nonmaterialistic culture of the Old South. Weaver especially treasured these lost civilizations as agrarian cultures with an "aristocracy of achievement" that—in the case of the Middle Ages and the Old South—submitted also to the "older religiousness" of Christianity and sustained individual dignity by viewing man as a craftsman. In *Ideas Have Consequences,* men who built the cathedrals of Europe are celebrated as craftsmen (as opposed to mere workers) who labored towards a great, spiritually fulfilling ideal. This stood opposed to Weaver's bleak view of the megalopolis where modern man wandered as a lost soul with no control of his economic destiny. Reduced to a mere economic unit, he now was a "slavey" in his office or factory at the mercy of impersonal corporations, monopolies, and industrialists.

The chivalry of the Middle Ages and the Old South was also much admired by Weaver. Men who "succored the helpless" and who "never turned on the enemy" were knights who protected a civilized order from those evil forces that will always be amongst us. The knight's duty had sentimental overtones. It was the sentiment of "big brother protecting little brother" that formed the real basis of human relationships. The doctrine of "undefined equality" on the other hand, only served to destroy such sentiments by declaring that diversity of personalities cannot exist.

Not surprisingly, Weaver viewed the French Revolution and the American Civil War as events resulting in equally catastrophic results for the West. Both revolutions destroyed the last vestiges of agrarian, feudal societies in Europe and North America. Both paved the way for the centralized state to control the economies and social life of culturally distinct communities. The Civil War, moreover, introduced the world to the doctrines of "total war" and unconditional surrender. For Weaver, total war represented the final fatal blow to the West's civilized order. A government which waged indiscriminate warfare against foreign enemies was also likely to deny individual liberties to its own citizens. The total warfare of the Civil War, Weaver claimed, also paved the way for even greater destruction in the world wars of the twentieth century. In *Visions of Order*, he drew the line from the total war policies of Sherman and Sheridan to the wholesale genocide of World War II, further predicting—with stunning accuracy—that such catastrophies "ensured future holocausts." This point of view has been echoed elsewhere, but it was hardly a prescription for a popular reception in mid-twentieth-century America. It was, however, the truth as Weaver saw it, and so he continued on that path.[4]

But even before those two events, the West was in a deep crisis, one brought about by the rise of nominalism and science in the fourteenth century and the subsequent rejection of a Higher Being. The belief in the transcendentals—or the Higher Being—provided the necessary humility for men to learn that life is a "matter of discipline and forging." Science, nominalism, and its offsprings, especially materialism, all inspired Western man to now act as his own "priest and ethics professor" with each new age bringing forth enough material progress as to render the passing age a backward epoch from which nothing can be learned. Looking at the industrial revolution he helped bring to America, Henry Ford gloried in the prosperity of the twentieth century and decided that "history is bunk." This sentiment—that the past is one large error and the present age represents the highest point of progress in human history—has turned man into a "moral idiot," a spoiled child who believes the life of prosperity and freedom is a birthright. Modern man has rejected the lessons of history, with its tales of man's limitations and tragedies. As a rootless, materialistic being, he also cuts himself off from the traditions of his ancestors. With nothing to link father and son, with man—in Allen Tate's famous phrase—"beginning each day as if there was no yesterday," he plunged into the future with excessive pride and egotism. A false view of man and history followed, explained by Weaver most memorably in his chapters "The Great Stereopticon" and "Egotism In Work And Art" from *Ideas Have Consequences*.[5]

Richard Weaver was especially alarmed by the acceptance of man as simply a "naturally good" creature. In his essay "Contemporary Southern Literature" Weaver quoted an anonymous Southern philosopher who, looking at the new doctrines from New England, remarked that "the theory of the natural goodness of man will blow up any society which it is founded on." The view of man as naturally good took no account of original sin or the existence of evil; thus it seemed impossible that any such society could defeat man's tendency towards evil. The question, What is man? is, of course, an ancient one, but still one that must be wrestled with by the poets and philosophers of every generation. Rather than seeing man as naturally good, or as seeing all men as being created equally, Weaver preferred the dual view of man—most dramatically portrayed in the fiction of William Faulkner, Robert Penn Warren, Thomas Wolfe, and other contemporary Southern novelists—and the more somber idea that "no man was born free and no two men were created equally."

If this vision of man seems obvious, we must remember that Weaver wrote in an age which championed the worth of the common man—and then created huge, centrally run bureaucracies to keep him in his place. In the 1940s, George Orwell declared that "we have now sunk to a depth at which the restatement of the obvious is the first duty of civilized men." This Weaver did in a relentless style, attacking in book after book, in essay after essay, the competing ideologies of his time. For instance, even more than statism, there was the secular religion of science. With science in the saddle, man could now conquer nature, master a world he did not make and live a life of ease and comfort without having to work very hard to maintain it. Weaver rejected false utopias; he especially exhorted modern man to say no to the social welfare state and instead opt for a more strenuous and courageous life. With examples from ancient Greece and Rome to feudal Europe and finally, to the early American civilization in New England and the South, Weaver championed the farmer, the man of the soil as a virtuous man fit for the responsibilities of freedom.

The dual view of man also offered hope even in civilization's darkest hours. Man is an angel, he is a monster. He is imbedded with original sin, a condition that he must constantly struggle to resist. Man is also—as Weaver often cited Alexander Pope—a creature wonderfully wrapped up in a "riddle, engima and joy." He was a creature capable of brave and noble deeds. As the knights of the Middle Ages rescued Europe from the abyss of rampant murder, rapine and chaos, so can men of every generation save their civilization from suicide. Yet Weaver was certainly no Pollyanna. He accused the scientific-technological order as promoting, through the mass media ("stereopticon" in Weaver's term), an "hysterical optimism" that refused to take into account the decadence of modern life. This refusal to submit to a false optimism also makes Weaver such a satisfying philosopher.

In all, eight books, including one textbook and three collections of essays, were published by Richard Weaver. Five books were published after his death in 1963. In a twenty-year career, Weaver also published 115 book reviews, essays and pamphlets, mostly in *National Review, Commonweal, Modern Age, Sewanee Review, Georgia Review, Virginia Quarterly*, and other scholarly publications. His textbook, *Composition: A Course in Reading and Writing*, was published in 1957 and revised ten years later. This study will concentrate on the published books and begins with a discussion of *The Southern Tradition at Bay*, a book published in 1968, nearly a quarter century after the author completed its first draft. *The Southern Tradition at Bay* was Richard Weaver's first book, a study that helped to form his worldview and one that also contained a searing criticism of modern life by Southern apologists that Weaver would soon make his own.

The contrast between the last days of the agrarian South as dramatized in *The Southern Tradition at Bay* and the chaos of urban life as portrayed in *Ideas Have Consequences* is vivid enough. From there, this study moves to *The Ethics of Rhetoric*, Weaver's *tour de force* through the world of rhetoric, from the "spaciousness" of the older and more visionary early American rhetoric to the intimidating "ultimate terms" of contemporary rhetoric, which bred cynicism and alienation amongst the masses. The later chapters examine Weaver's worth as a conservative theorist and defender of modern Southern culture to his final critique of modern society in *Visions of Order*, the final leg of a trilogy that began with *Ideas Have Consequences* and *Ethics of Rhetoric*. But first a short biographical note detailing the intellectual odyssey of this most private contemporary American philosopher.

1

Philosopher from Dixie

When Richard Weaver took his stand for an agrarian culture he was also defending his own family's long and hard-fought heritage. Although he spent the winters and autumns of his adult life in Chicago, Weaver, as soon as the last spring term paper was graded, took the train home to Weaverville, North Carolina where he would spend the summer plowing his patch of ancestral farmland while also working on his essays, reviews, and book-length projects.

As the reader may surmise, Weaverville was a town named for our subject's ancestors. The first Weaver who settled in western North Carolina emigrated east from Tennessee in the late eighteenth century, a few short years after the end of the Revolutionary War. John and Elizabeth Weaver became the first white settlers in an area ten miles north of Asheville, then known as Dry Ridge. John Weaver eventually came to own thousands of acres of property throughout the mountains of western North Carolina as both the Weaver family and the settlement grew in population. The town itself is named for Montraville Weaver, who donated land that would become the site of Weaver College, the area's first institution of higher learning.[1]

One family member especially caught Richard Weaver's imagination. To understand the culture into which Weaver was born and to also understand his own family's—and early America's—deep and unyielding agrarian roots, let us look at an address Weaver delivered to one of his family's annual summer reunions, occasions dubbed the meeting of the Tribe of Jacob. There, in 1954, Weaver eulogized his uncle Ethan Douglas Weaver, who had died the previous spring at age ninety-seven. Uncle Doug had farmed in Weaverville his entire adult life and along with his wife, raised a family of ten children. To his famous nephew, Uncle Doug's long life was proof of "great mental and spiritual health" in an age when "so many people are killing themselves with worry and indulgence." He was also remembered as a citizen of the Old Republic, living in Thomas Jefferson's America of independent farmers constituting the backbone of a free nation:

> In the whole course and tenor of his life, Uncle Doug suggests strongly the ideal citizen as he was contemplated, near the founding of this republic, by Thomas Jefferson. He was an agrarian; living on the soil; a primary producer creating things, not trafficking in the things that other men made. . . . In that spirit of independence which we associate with the builders of this country, he believed that the individual should support the state and not the state the individual. Again like a good Jeffersonian, he viewed politics with the watchful eye of the self-sustaining citizen; and many of us will recall the pithy and shrewd letters which he wrote to the local paper after he was well in his ninth decade. . . . There was much in his life to inspire those who cherish the early American ideals and much to rebuke those who have succumbed to easy ways and short-cut solutions.
>
> There was also much in this life to vindicate the agrarian type of society, with its wholesomeness, its rhythms in unison with nature, and its rooted strength. What an extraordinary thing it is in this age . . . for a man to sit on his own porch and watch the shade tree he planted with his own hands grow for sixty years! This it was Uncle Doug's privilege to do, and we feel right in saying that it was an earned privilege. In a world where so much is superficial, aimless and even hysterical, he kept a grasp upon those values which are neither old-fashioned nor new-fashioned but are central, permanent, and certain in their reward.[2]

The eldest of four children, Weaver's early life was upset by the death of his father, Richard Weaver Sr., which occurred when the younger Weaver was only six years old. Weaver's formative years were spent in Lexington, Kentucky. During the summer, he was sent home to Weaverville to enjoy those vacation months with his many relatives. Weaver's mother was heir to a Lexington family which operated a fairly prosperous millinery business that allowed the broken family to maintain a degree of financial security during the harsh Depression years. Like many writers, Weaver displayed bookish habits at an early age. His younger sister, Polly, remembers her older brother constantly being alone in his room, writing for hours on the family typewriter. Furthermore, Weaver's mother, Carrie recognized her son's intellectual potential and sent him to the Academy of Lincoln Memorial Prep School across the border in Harrogate, Tennessee. At Lincoln Memorial, Weaver formed, with two other students, a philosophy club that called for each member to contribute "something serious and significant" at each weekly meeting. Lincoln Memorial was not a prep school for the wealthy classes. During his entire time there, Weaver helped to pay for his tuition by working at the school cafeteria.[3]

Although Weaver was born into the rich agrarian tradition of yeoman farmers, he began his own intellectual odyssey as a man of the Left. Weaver's socialism was not something felt strongly in his bones. It was exclusively a product of his times. He became a socialist at a time when that ideology was usually the only one available to young people at college campuses throughout the country.

After graduating from Lincoln Memorial, Weaver matriculated at the University of Kentucky. Like most young people, Weaver had no developed positions, no guiding principles. Thus he was susceptible to the professors at Kentucky, whom he described years later as mostly "earnest souls" from the Midwest who were also "with or without knowing it, social democrats." The young undergraduate had "no defenses whatever against their doctrine." So in his precarious undergraduate years, Weaver had been "persuaded entirely that the future was with science, liberalism, and equalitarianism."[4]

After graduation, he even served as secretary of the local Socialist party. Through it all, Weaver remained an excellent student and debater. He chose English as a major, studied German and Spanish, and was elected Phi Beta Kappa. A classmate, Clifford Amyx, recalled many years later in a delightful essay, "Weaver The Liberal: A Memoir" that the young Weaver, far from his later public persona as a gloomy, studious scholar, was in most respects an average collegian (of that era) who enjoyed late night carousings where he was "utterly human and joyful." Amyx and Weaver also reviewed books and magazines for the student paper. Amyx recalls his friend printing a notice about the recently published agrarian manifesto, *I'll Take My Stand*, which the author correctly noted was a precursor of where Weaver's future would eventually take him.[5]

Indeed, Weaver's next stop was Vanderbilt University in Nashville. There he secured a teaching fellowship to help him study towards a Master's degree and a Ph.D. When the Kentuckian arrived at Vanderbilt, it was the nerve center of Southern Agrarian thought. John Crowe Ransom, Donald Davidson and John Donald Wade held posts in the English Department. Frank Owsley was teaching his groundbreaking interpretation of Southern history, while Lyle Lanier was in the Philosophy Department. Allen Tate, along with his wife, the novelist Caroline Gordon, was living and writing at a farm in nearby Clarksville. There the Agrarians often met to socialize and plan their next offensives (in those heady days after *I'll Take My Stand*, the Agrarians often referred to each other as "General"). Weaver was especially influenced by Ransom, who in the early 1930s was the most accomplished poet and critic among the soon-to-be famous Agrarian literary figures (this group also included *Stand* contributors Robert Penn Warren and Andrew Nelson Lytle). Not only an inspiring teacher of poetry, Ransom was also, according to Weaver, a "profound psychologist." Ransom had an uncanny talent for shedding new light on traditional ideas then under assault in an age of science and technology. "Long after the date of a lecture," Weaver recalled, "[You] would find some remark of his troubling you with its pregnancy and you would set about your own reflections upon it, after wishing that you had the master at hand to give another piece of insight." Weaver was further influenced by Ransom's 1930 book, *God Without Thunder*, the "unorthodox defense of orthodoxy" which eventually convinced Weaver that traditionalism could be defended in a time of rampant materialism. "I began to perceive," Weaver later wrote, "that many traditional positions in our world had suffered not so much because of inherent defects as because of stupidity, ineptness and intellectual sloth of those who for one reason or another were presumed to have their defense in charge."[6]

Ransom and the general Agrarian influence shook up the young Weaver's socialist presumptions, if not completely bringing him around to traditionalism. Weaver liked the Agrarians as persons. He especially was attracted to their acceptance of regional cultures, the folk arts, and social classes. All this contrasted dramatically with the egalitarian world view of his socialist mates, one that opposed the integrity of regional cultures, while romanticizing the invisible "mass man" living in a world made safe by the welfare state.

Weaver left Vanderbilt in 1936, short of gaining his Ph.D. He spent the next four years teaching, first for a year at Alabama Polytechnic Institute (now Auburn University) and then three years at Texas A & M. Weaver was generally unhappy in Texas. It seems he did little writing during his stint in Lubbock. Instead, the young bachelor spent weekends in Houston, regularly visiting local honky tonks and in general, enjoying the single life. But away from his natural calling,

Weaver's career was drifting nowhere. One day, he had enough. Driving to a job he disliked, Weaver realized he was still young enough to ditch this particular teaching job and "start his education all over." Which he did. In 1940, Weaver enrolled at Louisiana State University where he would finally earn his Ph.D. The Agrarian influence had won out over the socialism of his youth.

At LSU, Weaver settled down to complete a dissertation he had started earlier at Vanderbilt. He embarked on an enormous research of the postbellum literature of the defeated South with an emphasis on the men who fought the epic struggles of the Civil War. With total warfare raging across Europe and Asia, Weaver discovered the virtues of chivalry, the "older religiousness," and the idea of a responsible aristocracy as essential to any civilized community. The dissertation, entitled "The Confederate South 1865–1910: A Study in the Survivial of a Mind and Culture," was, as we have already noted, not published until 1968. While teaching at North Carolina State University in 1943, Weaver edited and rewrote sections of the dissertation. He then submitted the manuscript to the University of North Carolina Press. The editors at Chapel Hill turned down the book. However, the dissertation achieved a solid reputation in the academic world and was enough to secure Weaver a position at the University of Chicago's College Department of English. Weaver moved to Chicago in 1944 and spent the rest of his professional career there.[7]

Throughout his works, Richard Weaver called on modern man to reject the trappings of the social welfare state and opt, instead, for the strenuous life. From his time in Chicago, we can affirm that Weaver certainly practiced what he preached. His breakthrough came in 1948 when the University of Chicago Press elected to publish *Ideas Have Consequences*. Although the book received a large critical reception and for a philosophical study, sold well, the Chicago hierarchy viewed Weaver with considerable suspicion. William T. Couch, the director of the press was fired from his post several years later and Weaver had to look elsewhere to find publishers for future works.[8]

Still, he carried on. Weaver was a dedicated teacher; from his days as a teaching fellow at Vanderbilt to his unhappy tenure at Texas A & M to the more invigorating atmosphere in Chicago, teaching was the only professional job he held. Weaver's experience led him to write several insightful essays lamenting the decline of quality in American education—and even the dubious idea of mass education itself. Teaching was a profession Weaver held in great esteem. In "To Write The Truth," an essay that was collected in *Language is Sermonic*, Weaver wrote that the teacher must be someone with supreme knowledge who also brings the "sword of division" into the classroom, defining good and evil, right and wrong. Weaver's battle was against the rise of relativism, a doctrine that, among other things, held that no one student can hold superior gifts to the next. In addition, distinctions of age, class, and sex were deemed nonexistent. If teachers do not really possess superior knowledge, if giving out grades is undemocratic, then choosing professors at the University of Chicago (or anywhere else) would, as Weaver dryly noted, be an easy task. One could simply go to Soldier's Field in Chicago, and draw pieces from a large kettle. All those who draw blue slips will be our teachers for the coming semester. Those with other colors will presumably sit out the term. In addition to his other accomplishments, Weaver was one of the first great post-World War II critics of the triumphant, John Dewey-influenced egalitarian approach to education.

Even after he became an established author, Weaver insisted on teaching a freshman English composition course each year to incoming students. Freshman composition is regarded as the type of labor a professor hopes to eventually be liberated from doing, yet Weaver taught it throughout his entire time at Chicago. He argued that far more than being a "skills" course, it was in fact, a course whose content was rhetoric—with rhetoric itself always being "the key to a liberal education." Weaver taught rhetoric to his freshmen so they would realize that although dialectic, the definition of things, is important, a persuasive and visionary rhetoric must be added to a definition in order to give an argument staying power. An honest rhetoric moves men towards noble goals and Weaver defended the teaching of composition courses on these grounds.[9]

Along with his teaching responsibilities, Weaver wrote seven days a week, writing first drafts of reviews, essays and books in longhand and later typing the final draft on carbon paper. Weaver was friendly enough with his colleagues in the English Department. Like Clifford Amyx, Wilma Ebbitt remembers Weaver as a man who enjoyed a drink, a good joke, popular folk songs, and the company of pretty women. But for the most part, Weaver lived a reclusive life in Chicago. Edward Shils, a longtime member of the university's Sociology Department, recalled while receiving the 1989 Richard M. Weaver

Award for Scholarly Letters, that Weaver was a solitary figure on campus, a man engaged in a struggle against much of modernism and not at all part of the several highly optimistic pro-New Deal cliques that existed then on the Chicago campus.

Whether Weaver liked Chicago is not terribly important. We have several varying opinions on the matter and either way, his years in the Windy City were productive ones. The university itself gave him great intellectual stimulus. Polly Weaver Beaton recalled that it allowed Weaver to match wits, debate and socialize with other serious thinkers. Polly's husband, Kendall Beaton recalled that Weaver disliked city life, but added that Chicago did give the exiled Southerner an affiliation to one of the more renowned universities in the Western world. Being at a Northern university was a normal situtation for Southern conservatives such as Richard Weaver. Fred Hobson noted that the Southern disapora to the North followed by Weaver, Tate, Warren, Brooks, Ransom, and others was the natural course for Southern Agrarians who found universities in their home region increasingly in the hands of progressives and thus hostile to a traditionalist philosophy. Northern universities, hence, were more open in their own right. They recruited and tolerated Southern intellecutals who were thoroughly (by choice) out of step with the reigning liberalism of the 1930s, 40s, 50s and early 60s. Near the end of his career, Weaver was invited back to Vanderbilt. There he would take Donald Davidson's chair for one semester. Davidson was nearing retirement and the invitation, as Walter Sullivan tells it, was meant as the first step towards securing a permanent position for Weaver at Vanderbilt. Indeed, Weaver once told Wilma Ebbitt that Vanderbilt was the only university in America preferrable to Chicago. Eventually, Weaver intended to retire to Weaverville, to a new home bought with money saved from his teaching career where away from the university, he would continue a life dedicated to scholarship.[10]

But "that earned retreat" as Marion Montgomery termed it, from Weaver's "battles in the outer jungles of modernism," never came. In April, 1963, Weaver died suddenly of a heart attack in his South Side Chicago hotel room. It was, as Fred Hobson described it, a "bleak death for any man, one more befitting an inhabitant of Eliot's Waste Land than a loyal son of the rural South." Russell Kirk eulogized Weaver as inspiring the revival of conservatism in America and similar tributes were paid throughout the years. Nineteen sixty-four saw the release of *Visions of Order* and as already noted, the subsequent years saw more posthumous publications. There was also the establishment of the heretofore mentioned Weaver Fellowships and the Weaver Award for Scholarly Letters. "Weaver had sowed deep his intellectual seed," Kirk wrote of his friend and mentor, "and although he left no heirs of his body, the heirs of his mind may be many and stalwart."[11]

There have been many heirs to Weaver's traditionalism, but not nearly as many as Kirk and other conservatives would have hoped for. A philosopher who goes against the the grain of modern thought, who does not necessarily believe that the current age is superior to the past (that is, not properly "progressive"), will always have difficulty gaining a positive critical and public reception. Weaver's disciples remain a defiant minority within the conservative intellecutal community. Kirk and M.E. Bradford are gone, but others in the same "paleoconservative" tradition—Clyde Wilson, J.O. Tate, Thomas Fleming, Paul Gottfried, Chilton Williamson, Jr., Samuel Francis, Joseph Sobran, George Panichas, Marion Montgomery, Thomas Landess—remain an unreconstructed and unreconstrutable band of writers and thinkers attempting to forge a new conservatism based on the foundations of the Old Republic. Even a feisty minority with unshakeable convictions may influence the trend of mainstream politics—a position which Weaver's followers find themselves in today. Recognizing that Richard Weaver was a private man, a hard worker, and a serious teacher, it is now time to look at our subject's enduring body of work.[12]

2

An Aristocracy of Achievement:
The Southern Tradition at Bay

The Southern Tradition at Bay is divided into two sections, the first is a concise explanation of the heritage of the Old South and the second, following that society's military defeat, details its spirited attempts to preserve the heritage by a diverse and sometimes frantic group of apologists. Traditionalists such as Weaver were forever being accused of trying to "turn back the clock." Weaver answered those charges throughout his work, adding in one essay that he was only trying to "set the clock right." Charges of being a reactionary are never greater than when one takes up a defense of the Old South. Weaver's thesis was that from the Old South we supremely confident moderns can learn "something of how to live."

So what *can* we learn from the Old South? In short, Weaver admired the Old South as an outpost of feudal Europe in an age when Europe itself had moved on to a more secular, egalitarian society and the rest of North America had followed suit. Holding on to virtues of feudal Europe, the Old South was "the last non-materialistic civilization in the Western world," one where manners, morals, and codes of conduct mattered more than mere moneymaking. That is the crux of the book.

The heart of the thesis comes in pages 96–395, when Weaver chronicles the Southern reaction to the shock of defeat. But before making that study, Weaver introduces the reader to the Old South, specifically to the world the landed gentry made. The heritage of the

Old South, to Weaver, is a solid antidote to the crass materialism, the ceaseless human competition, the dehumanizing forces of our time. Consider this favorable comparison of the feudal order to the "envy and hatred" of our modern-day money culture:

> The relative self-sufficiency of the plantation . . . the sense of kinship with the soil, present too in its humbler inhabitants, who felt pangs on leaving "the old place"—these were the supports of Southern feudalism. . . . It possessed stability, an indispensable condition for positive values: it maintained society in the only true sense of the term, for it had structure and articulation, and it made possible a personal world in which people were known by their names and their histories. It was a rooted culture which viewed with dismay the anonymity and the social indifference of urban man.[1]

There were four aspects to the heritage—the feudal system, the code of chivalry, the education of the gentleman, and the older religiousness. Weaver saw shortcomings in the education; not enough emphasis was placed on literature and the life of letters, even if practiced by a Poe or a Simms, was considered a relatively useless occupation, or at best, something a man would do for only a few years of his life. Being a man of action, the Southerner tended towards a life in politics or to mastering the soldierly arts.

Other than that, Weaver heartily approved of the heritage. All aspects are out of favor today—and have been since the passing of the Middle Ages. Weaver knew this, but he defended the heritage as a foundation for any civilized society. In the final three chapters of *Ideas Have Consequences*, Weaver laid out a plan of restoration for the modern world, one built around private property and a return to piety and honesty in the spoken and written word. But examples of the heritage presented here represent an even stronger alternative to the ills of modern life.

All aspects of the heritage were nonmaterialistic. In the Old South, the question was not the more modern: "How much are you worth?" but in the tradition of the ancient Greeks, it was "Where are you from? And where are you headed?" Or as Calvin S. Brown put it: "A gentleman may be aware that a man may have two million dollars and not be worth two cents."[2] Furthermore, all aspects of the heritage are *interesting* to the modern reader—especially to any native of the "New South" that emerged in the 1960s and 70s. Just the claim that we can learn from the Old South is bold enough. We have long been told there is nothing worth saving from the old regime; it only represented a great evil in American history. Weaver doesn't deny that pettiness and brutality existed in the South, he is only asking that the "liberal arts" live up to their lofty claims, that we give the Old South a fair reading in history. And so the first ninety-three pages of the book are chock full of Old South virtues.

Consider the code of chivalry. Weaver knew that our age, with its awesome technological prowess and ability to wage total war that wipes out and humilitates the enemy, could not appreciate this vital characteristic of the Old South. But chivalry was serious business to Richard Weaver. The knight of the Middle Ages was the heroic figure who restored civilization to the European continent. His actions saved Europe from the dark night of barbarism that followed the death of Charlemagne. The knight stood as civilization's last line of defense. Indeed, the whole code encompasses courage, brotherhood, and duty. The knight must never "turn on the enemy." He exists to "speak the truth" and protect the helpless. The knight understood war will never end. At best, however, conflicts can be contained if we only make war on armed men. Once the war ends, the victor showed his magnanimity by welcoming the losing side into the brotherhood of nations. In short, no civilized order can exist without the spirit of chivalry.

Likewise, the feudal system spawned a paternalism that Weaver also claimed held great relevance for the modern world. Like the knight, the gentleman had a sense of noblesse oblige. But it was much different from our sense of the word. We have our own elites; we also have a hostile view of them. Far from being natural leaders, they are seen as scheming, devious players in the "global economy" who care little for the plight of the working classes. Twentieth-century America had its aristocratic families: the Roosevelts, the Kennedys, the Rockefellers, the Bushes. Members of those families entered politics, but their idea of noblesse oblige is quite different from their eighteenth- and nineteenth-century predecessors. It has usually meant creating social programs through enormous transfers of monies from one class to another. Granted, this is a cynical view, but the old-style gentleman did not need or want a Leviathan state. A benign paternalism existed in the South both before and after the Civil War. For a Washington, a Jefferson, a John Randolph of Roanoke, it meant taking care of his help when they were sick, bailing them out of jail, introducing them to Christianity.

Weaver put great emphasis on the art of subtlety. Thus he opens

The Southern Tradition at Bay by quoting Jose Ortega y Gasset: "The simple process of preserving our present civilization is supremely complex and demands incalculaby subtle powers." Here Weaver practices that rare talent. He maintained that the gentleman was concerned with the dignity of the individual. The paternal tradition also meant training each man in a profession—carpenter, shoemaker, blacksmith, tanner, spinner, weaver, currier. "With such diversity of occupation," Weaver noted, "there was a task adpated to everyone and when a worker grew too old for a certain kind of employment, he would be shifted, in paternalistic fashion, to another better suited to his condition." The point is that both a responsible hierarchy and Christian charity does a better job of "succoring the helpless" and uplifting the less fortunate than an impersonal Leviathan state built by the devotees of social engineering.[3]

At the same time he was working on his dissertation, Weaver was also reconsidering the agnosticism of his youth. As a socialist and a believer in science, egalitarianism and the superiority of the state, Weaver admitted he had no use for religion. The whole idea of original sin—when it was clear man could be saved by state programs and scientific progress—seemed far-fetched and rather comical to the young scholar. But after witnessing the destruction wrought by the doctrine of total war, the young Weaver suddenly found modern man well in need of the humility one obtains through religion. The saving grace of Christianity was its simple message of original sin, a phenomenon which alone explains the fearful levels of barbarism that raged throughout the twentieth century. Original sin was simply "a parabolical expression of the immemorial tendency of man to do the wrong thing when he knows the right thing." In a world that denied original sin, Weaver looked to the religion of the Old South as an antidote to this dangerous arrogance.[4]

In his famous essay "Remarks on the Southern Religion" from *I'll Take My Stand,* Allen Tate found the Old South lacking in its spiritual life. "They had a religious life," Tate observed, "but it was not enough organized with a right mythology." Tate's own journey would lead him into the Catholic Church; perhaps such a regime could have saved the South. Weaver would agree with Tate on the South's inability to "perfect its world view" and that such a failure carried far more damage than defeats on a battlefield. But it appears Weaver would disagree with Tate on the religious aspect of Southern culture.[5]

Weaver saw little to criticize in the older religiousness. Indeed one can argue that this aspect of the heritage has survived in the Sunbelt South. In the early decades of the twentieth century, W.J. Cash declared the South to be the world's last outpost of Christendom. Weaver might not have agreed with Cash on other matters (Cash, for one, had a dim view of the South's aristocratic heritage), but like Cash, Weaver admired the South for holding onto the ideals of Christian Europe long after Europe (and New England) had generally denied the existence of a vengeful God. Even today, as the Bible Belt, or headquarters of the dreaded religious right, the South's enduring faith in the older religiousness continues to hold the nation's somewhat bemused attention. Here and in other essays on the South, Weaver makes a rousing defense of the Southern religion—which is especially noteworthy since Weaver himself was not very religious. He only attended church services once a year. According to Russell Kirk, an Episcopalian high mass offered during the Christmas season provided Weaver with enough emotional satisfication to last the rest of the year.[6]

What did Southerners want from religion? For one, religion needed to be a fufilling experience. Churchgoers needed fire and brimstone services; they accepted a jealous God who punishes sinners. Southerners also took a strong belief in the idea of a divine Providence; all earthly events were guided by God's hand. Certain things in this world must remain a mystery. Not everything can be solved by man's ingenuity. Nature was God's creation, something for man to both contend with and enjoy. It was not a vast wasteland for us to conquer and exploit.

The older religion also had a correct view of man. This creature had a dual nature; he wasn't by any means, a "naturally good" being. Instead, he was a sinner who fell from grace in the Garden of Eden. This world, Southerners believed, was not a utopia; no amount of scientific or technological refinement could make it so. Religion was a settled affair meant for the "inner conversion" of man. Weaver's characterizations of the older religiousness contains some of his best writing in the book.

It seems an inescapable inference that in the sphere of religion the Southerner has never been friendly to the spirit of inquiry. He felt, with what may now appear prophetic instinct, that religion which is intellectual only is no religion. . . . Whether he was a Virginia Episcopalian, dozing in comfortable dogmatic slumber, or a Celt, transplanted to the Appalachian wilderness and responding to the wild emotionalism of the religious rally, he wanted the older religiousness of dreams and drunkenness—something akin to the rituals of the Medieval Church, and to the Eleusinian mysteries of the ancients.[7]

Best of all, when it came to religion, Southerners were a highly tolerant people. For instance, there was little of the anti-Catholic sentiments that accompanied early Catholic immigration into the United States. Religious tolerance flourished in the South because Southerners respected any religion that preached salvation through obedience; for Weaver, this marked the appearance of a disciplined people.

Religion was also a source of tension—one of the first such tensions—between the mind of New England and the mind of the South. As strong believers, Southerners were highly suspicious of skeptical people, especially on religious matters. Skeptical people could not live orderly, disciplined lives. Worst of all, as Weaver noted, skeptical people were forever making war against people "whose idea of right did not comport with their own." Increasingly, New England theologians saw religion as an engine of political upheaval while the South continued to view religion strictly as a means of personal salvation. Hence, the rise of the abolitionists and the beginning of tensions and suspiciousness that ignited the most terrible fuse in Amerian history.

In defending the education of the gentleman, Weaver had plenty of firepower on hand, namely, he could point to the men who made the first republic of the modern world. There was Thomas Jefferson, author of the Declaration of Independence and James Madison, still identified here as the celebrated author of the U.S. Constitution. These are the obvious figures. But there was also Patrick Henry, John Randolph of Roanoke and John Taylor of Caroline, men who jealously guarded the decentralizing tenets of the Constitution (indeed, Randolph broke with Henry and later Jefferson when he maintained those gentlemen had strayed from their original states' rights positions).

All were products of Virginia, the commonwealth where the education flourished to historic heights. In brief, education served to cultivate "the whole man." A man was educated in the liberal arts, literature, philosophy, classical languages, rhetoric, as well as in science and mathematics. Most of all, he was educated to be a leader of men in both times of war and times of peace. The reader may recall Henry ("Light-Horse Harry") Lee's eulogy of George Washington. No matter what his profession might be, the gentleman was educated to become an heir to five thousand years of Western culture. The education also provided for a broad understanding of human nature. A belief in false utopias, experiments in social engineering, and other dogmas inspired by science would not become part of the education. In short, the education flourished in an era when the purpose of the university was to produce Christian gentlemen.[8]

Weaver is most convincing when he makes the case that Washington and Robert E. Lee were products of what was good and noble about the education of the gentleman. Although social malcontents of our time have taken their culture war to attacking the legends of both men, most Americans continue to hold strong sentimental feelings towards Washington and Lee. Their examples add plenty of luster to Weaver's brief for the Old South.

Washington did not have the formal education of Jefferson or Madison, but through courage on the battlefield in the service of the British crown, he became part of the landed gentry. A man of wealth and considerable landholdings, Washington was willing to risk his vast possessions by taking up arms against the same crown he once defended. During the Revolutionary War, the aristocrat suffered with his troops at Valley Forge and through numerous defeats on the battlefield. But in the tradition of the knight, he never did turn from the enemy, eventually prevailing in the historic eight-year struggle. In the tradition of the gentleman, he led in times of war and of peace. When the new republic called on him to be its first president, the reluctant statesman served for eight years; then, like a modern-day Cincinnatus, he gratefully returned back to the land to cultivate his fig and vine tree. Washington was proof that an aristocracy could avoid petrification by recruiting from the yeoman classes.

Possibly because his trials were greater, Lee, even more so than Washington, is presented by Weaver and others as the *beau ideal* of Southern civilization. In the early American tradition, Lee was a provincial. He was also a sterling example that the concrete bonds of blood and land were more important to nineteenth-century Americans than abstract ideals like democracy, equality, or even "Union." Quoting the general's great biographer, Douglas Southall Freeman, Weaver wrote that once Lee plowed the Virginia earth, he had felt a "oneness with her." And even after being offered command of Union troops on the eve of the Civil War, Lee could not take up arms against his native state. Lee also displayed the finest virtues of chivalry. During the invasion of Pennsylvania, he issued strict orders for his troops not to harm women and children, but only to make war against armed men.

Weaver, like others, especially revered Lee's behavior in the dreadful reconstruction era that followed the war. Despite his Confederate sympathies, Weaver also was an admirer of Abraham Lincoln. In his 1944 essay, "Lee the Philosopher," Weaver saw the general as the man who would carry out the reconciliation process between the two regions that Lincoln had promised to oversee. Lee's private thoughts, published later in biographies and memoirs, contained plenty of bitterness, but the public Lee was calm and reasoned, urging reconciliation and predicting an eventual end to reconstruction.

As the years went on, Lee was well on his way to becoming one of the most popular and respected figures in the reunited nation. Northern editorialists sang his praises, held him up as an example, and urged readers to contribute funds to Washington College in Lexington, Virginia, where Lee served as president. A Democratic party newspaper in New York City even called on that party, in 1867, to nominate Lee for the presidency of the United States. Lee's tenure at Washington College soon became legendary. There he educated young men for one stated purpose: To become Christian gentlemen. He would accept no federal monies for the university, but he added new courses, such as engineering and journalism (the Civil War had spawned a tremendous increase in newspaper readers in Amerca) to prepare young men for a changing world. He urged his fellow Southerners to once again become Americans.

Before the war, Lee was a Unionist who had bitterly opposed the Deep South's secession. During the conflict, he came around to the same secessionist position with the same passion—a view he never recanted in the postwar years. But his sterling example of patriotism was a major factor in swinging public opinion against the Radical Republicans. In 1876, a Democrat, Samuel Tilden won the popular vote count in the presidential election. The electoral college vote remained unclear for weeks following the election. Tilden's election alone would bring down the curtain on both Radical Republicanism and carpetbag rule in the South. However, the ruling Republicans were able to steal the election by making a deal with the Democratic South which basically said: Allow us to elect Rutherford Hayes and we will both withdraw our troops from the South and leave you people alone to solve your social problems.

Lee's genius, according to Weaver, was to "counsel reconciliation in a manner that stood outside the passion of the times." Over the course of the decade, many Northerners who had traveled South for quick business killings eventually saw the error of trying to impose carpetbag rule on the defeated region. Many Southerners, once they regained control of their states realized—as we will see with the discussion of Southern liberals—that they had to include the freedman in a program of progress. And so along with the infamous deal of 1876, the "first reconstruction," to the profound relief of statesmen on both sides, ended.[9]

The first section of *The Southern Tradition at Bay*, then, is mainly a homage to an aristocracy of achievement. The landed gentry followed Washington's dictum that a man must not only be virtuous, but must also give the appearance of virtue. For instance, money was never a discussion topic around the dinner table. The gentleman, moreover, was a wise, prudent man, with a keen understanding both of human nature and world history. M.E. Bradford, for one, always championed the U.S. Constitution as a document solidly grounded in human history. Rationalism, along with science, was one of the great dogmas of the eighteenth (and certainly nineteenth) century. The Founding Fathers preferred history, not reason, as the lodestar to writing that famous document. "Reason may mislead us," Bradford was fond of quoting John Dickinson, one of the more underrated Founding Fathers. So let history, with its countless examples of man's failings and glory, be our guide instead.[10]

As such, the gentleman lived in splendid isolation from the world's problems—which in itself was a goal of the Old Republic. There is George Washington's famous farewell speech imploring the nation not to be part of the "entangling alliances" that would eventually lead to endless warfare. Weaver cites an early Southern novelist who commented that life in Virginia was never so good as when her roads were bad. Even the steamboat, hardly an engine of industrialism run rampant, was considered an intrusion on the gentleman's world.

In this respect, the Southern tradition defined here by Richard Weaver was in fact the early American tradition shared also by many New Englanders. The gentleman's first allegiance was to his own state, county, sometimes merely to his own plot of land. In the English tradition, name and land were defining characteristics of a culture. For Weaver, this created a sense of stability, responsibility, dignity, and sentiment. The importance of name and place stood as safeguards against the whims of the political culture. The yeoman also saw his little red acre as the source of his allegiance; it was a sentiment he would fight and die for. The New England novelist Nathaniel Hawthorne understood such allegiances, contending that a "state was as large a territory as anyone could be expected to love, and that love for an invisible hypothesis like the American Union was something few people had the imagination to achieve."[11]

Furthermore, John Adams' hope that Americans would not be "avenging angels" seeking out foreign devils to conquer was a sentiment easily shared by Washington and Jefferson. In short, the gentleman understood that his young republic (or any nation) was not going to redeem a fallen world. Constitutional law and republican government could, however, create and sustain conditions for liberty. He would have rejected, as postbellum apologists did, the desire to embark on empire-building and "export the American idea" to all parts of the earth.

And so we have another major theme of *The Southern Tradition at Bay*: the fall of the gentleman was a catastrophe from which the South has never recovered. Not all twentieth-century Southern pols were rabble-rousers of the Theodore Bilbo, Cole Blease variety. Harry Byrd, Richard Russell, Walter George, John Stennis, and Coke Stevenson were, to name a few, certainly in the tradition Weaver admired. But in an age of industrialism and its most baneful creation, urban culture, a "raw, aggressive" democracy is inevitable. Doctrines such as states' rights—which were an outgrowth of the nation's founding agrarian culture—quickly became obsolete. In the twentieth century, nearly all Southern politicians were supporters of Franklin Roosevelt's New Deal: they wanted federal largess for their districts, but they also wanted the feds to leave the South's social arrangements alone. That was a strategy destined for failure. However, Weaver only dwells briefly on the shortcomings of the Southern tradition in his extended writings on his home region.[12]

Unreconstructed and Unreconstructable

That the heritage was admired and considered worth saving is affirmed in the book's second section. The final 300 pages provide the reader with colorful, passionate opinions from a remarkable cross-section of Southerners—soldiers, politicians, lawyers, journalists, educators—all of whom offered apologies for the region with some later giving criticism through social commentary, satire, and fiction.

In the bibliography, Weaver cites over 200 books, novels, reminiscences, and diaries as part of his scholarship. Only a few authors—Ellen Glasgow and Joel Chandler Harris to name two—have had any staying power. Some, especially Thomas Dixon, are more notorious than fondly remembered. But others, such as the anti-Lincoln critic Albert Taylor Bledsoe and the novelist Opie Read are elevated to their rightful places as important social commentators.

The feisty defense of the heritage proved to Weaver that, at least for a while, the Southern mind proved to be "unreconstructed and unreconstructable," representing a tough conservatism that might be a bulwark against the tide of modernity. By the end of the book, Weaver concluded that the entire effort had failed. Conservatives worshipped the past too much in its "crystallized form" and could not even adapt slightly to changing times. Liberals increasingly began to see the past as a "large error" and thus saw no need to preserve the heritage. In *Visions of Order*, Weaver wrote that the world does indeed change— "things are and are becoming"—but change does not call for ancient traditions and institutions to be destroyed. Certain distinctions—differences, for instance, between the sexes, those of youth and old age—cannot be tampered with.

By 1910, in Weaver's estimation, the region had ceased to be a "fighting South" and was tumbling down the road towards materialism. Weaver concluded that the South "never perfected a worldview." Its apologists were never able to "show why the South was right *finally*." In short, the South never defined or really understood its correct antimaterialistic position. But the people themselves were not listening to their prophets. After all, several well-written journals dedicated to the survival of Southern culture—such as Bledsoe's *Southern Bivowac*—were not supported by Southerners who preferred buying books and magazines published in New York—presumably because they represented correct thinking.

Still, the failure is not all the reader remembers about *The Southern Tradition at Bay*. In these pages, there is a portrait of a living, breathing South; a picture of real civilization, indeed, a real nation. There is a way of life based on the particularisms of culture, not solely on accumulation of material things. The culture had its own codes of conduct (chivalry), morals (the older religiousness), and a set of manners that allowed for a certain *demarche* between blacks and whites.

The South had a way of life, a sense of right and wrong. By bringing all of the apologists together in one last rebel yell, Weaver himself defines the Old South. He succeeds where these earlier apologists fell short. As Tom Landess notes, Weaver "has written a call to battle that we can ignore only at our peril, and he may have written the very work he calls for at the end of his long and rewarding study."[13]

While trying to live up to the heritage, the apologists leveled a blast at modernism itself, one that Weaver would emulate throughout his career. Indeed, what strikes the reader is the defiance of a people who were defeated on the battlefield, who lived under military occupation for a good decade after the war, and most of whom were stuck in deep poverty for years to come. Once the region that produced most of the nation's early presidents, soldiers, and statesmen, the South was now—and for several decades—no longer part of the political or economic power structure of the reunited nation. But their spirit was not yet broken. For an example of defiance, consider this character, a Reverend Durham, from Dixon's *The Leopard's Spots* speaking to his Boston counterpart about his homeland:

> I've studied your great cities. Believe me the South is worth saving. Against a possible day when a flood of foreign anarchy threatens the foundations of the Republic and men shall laugh at the faiths of your fathers, and undigested wealth beyond the dreams of avarice rots your society until it mocks at honor, love and God—against that day we will preserve the South.[14]

And Edwin Alderman, president of the University of Virginia, speaking to students at the University of California in 1868, suggests that the defeated South will rise again not only to save itself but the entire nation:

> And so when an age of moral warfare shall succeed to the age of passionate gain-getting; when blind social forces have wrought some tangle of inequality and of injustice, of hatred and suspicion, when calculation and combination can only weave the web more fiercely; when the whole people in some hour of national peril shall seek for the man of heart and faith, who will not falter or fail, in the sweet justice of God, hither shall they turn for succor as once they turned to a simple Virginia farmer.[15]

This section contributes mightily to our main thesis—what can we learn from the Old South? The efforts of the apologists are so compelling that it is incumbent we study several of them in depth.

Consider first, the Confederate soldier. Weaver's examples make it clear that no other Southern figure lived up the heritage as well as the man-in-arms. Various soldiers, in their memoirs, made the legal case for secession, but being men of action, their books were mostly tales that celebrated the thrill of combat. Considering the nation's new economic and political situation, the ex-soldier didn't have much else to look foward to. Heroic tales from the war occupied days spent around the town square, building, along with the many published books on the war, the kind of mythology of bravery and sacrifice that Weaver always claimed was essential in transmitting a recognizable culture from one generation to the next.

The reminiscences revealed soldiers, who far from believing "war is hell," had looked at the conflict as a great tournament. Like Washington and his Revolutionary War troops, the Confederate soldier did not turn from the enemy. Henry Douglas in *I Rode With Stonewall* recalls how sorry he felt for soldiers who were too sick or injured to fight on the front lines. Portraits of Stonewall Jackson, Jeb Stuart and John Pelham are etched in colorful prose. For John Esten Cooke, in the classic *Wearing of the Gray*, the death of Stuart was not a cause for commentary on the awfulness of war, but on the mythical prescence "The Last Cavalier" held on his men even as he was dying: "[H]e fell like some 'monarch of the woods' which makes the whole forest resound as it crashes down." Jackson, in his prime, is described thusly by Cooke: "In the man who holds aloft his hand in prayer while his veteran battalions move by steadily to the charge, it will not be difficult to fancy a reproduction of the stubborn Cromwell, sternest of Ironsides, going forth to conquer in the name of the Lord." Pelham's famous defense at Fredericksburg is described in equally mythic terms: "All know how stubbornly he stood on that day—what laurels encircled his young brow when night at last came."[16]

The common soldier loved the chieftain. The war, Weaver declared, only served to strengthen the bonds between the aristocrat and yeoman classes. The finest of the Southern aristocracy—Lee, Richard Taylor, A.P. Hill, Jubal Early—took to the field during the war. The civilian leadership showed little imagination, but in the field, the aristocrat performed admirably. During the war, the aristocrat and the yeoman farmer lived, fought, and died together. As Weaver noted with satisfication, the common soldier was happy with—and in fact, needed—an aristocracy of achievement. The soldier did not identify himself as a member of the "Georgia 14th Calvary" or the "Virginia 37th Infantry," but as a fighting man in "Lee's Army" or riding with "Old Jack." That the aristocrat was in the field, leading his charges into battle, only increased the yeoman's respect for the idea of a hierarchy. Such examples legitimized Weaver's place for the aristocrat as a natural leader of men and highlighted the need for some social classes as necessary for a civilized, tranquil society.

The soldier was also highly religious. During the war, tens of thousands converted to Christianity. After the war, their faith became even stronger. The defeat was a cause for soul-searching. Some Southerners analyzed the region's sins and shortcomings as reasons behind God's providence, but skepticism towards Christianity wasn't part of the debate. Weaver noticed that disillusionment set in only after the chieftain died or more profoundly, when the tactics of total war prevailed. For the Confederate soldier, war, in the tradition of the medieval knight, was seen as a test of one's manhood, bravery, and skill. Some Southerners were so naive about modern times as to think that when their boys won the first Battle of Manassas, the war was over. The South had proved its manhood, its will to fight on fields of honor. That in itself should have settled the issue. But there was no shame in losing an honest test of skills.

Only when war became a "business transaction" to be pursued by indiscriminate means, did the soldier begin to recognize the darker side of human nature. Admiral Raphael Semmes's bitter memoirs claimed the war proved that self-government was incapable of blunting man's evil nature. General Richard Taylor realized the great changes brought on by a policy of total warfare. This was more than just a way of conducting battles. The war helped change the definition and purpose of man. If war was a "business transaction," then domestic life would be operated the same way. Modern man in everyday life was now reduced to Weaver's dreaded economic unit, a creature good only as a consuming animal and a cog in the moneymaking culture.

Reflecting on these memoirs, Weaver saw the soldier as a man of wisdom, eloquently commenting on the passing of a way of life. The soldier, Weaver wrote, saw "that a change was passing over the nation, that something in the soul of the people was dying, that a pristine state of simplicity, likened to that of our first parents, was being destroyed by the forces of an active evil." Such turns in mood heightens the book's standing as an account of an authentic American tragedy.[17]

Later on, Weaver would also write that the soldier left a legacy of duty and chivalry that did his reunited nation plenty of good. The martial arts were popular in the South before the war, but the great conflict of the 1860s only intensified the Southern appetite for military valor. Decades later, during the Spanish-American war, startled Northerners were pleasantly surprised at the sight of Fitzhugh Lee (Robert E. Lee's nephew) and Fighting Joe Wheeler (he of Civil War cavalry fame) donning the blue and leading U.S. Army troops into action. During the hot days of the Cold War, Weaver predicted that the South— with all its grievances against the American Union—would nonethless rise again to lead the nation to victory over communism.

> With pragmatists and relativists giving away the free world bit by bit, his [the Southerner's] willingess to fight with an intransigent patriotism may be the one thing that can save the day from the darkness gathering in Eastern Europe and Asia. If that time should come, the nation as a whole would understand the spirit that marched with Lee and Jackson and charged with Pickett.[18]

And then there is the case of the Southern liberal and like-minded progressives.

For all his well-deserved reputation as one of the twentieth century's great foes of liberalism, Richard Weaver had some sympathy for that philosophy. Not the destructive twentieth-century variety that places all faith in the Leviathan state, but an earlier liberalism that stood for individual freedom and a very limited state role in the life of a community.

Most interesting is Weaver's reading of Henry Grady, the Atlanta orator and renowned founding father of the New South. Grady is identified with Southern liberalism, but Weaver finds him closer to the traditionalists. Here, Grady emerges as one who eagerly accepted the "social creeds of antebellum civilization." The South, Grady argued, should save its heritage because it represented the "last hope of saving the old-fashioned in our religious and political government."

Grady was a strong traditionalist. He championed the older religiousness, railing against the "bitterness of unbelief" that religious skeptics were nurturing. There was nothing wrong with a South that "has left us the straight and simple faith of our fathers, untained by heresy and unweakened by speculation." Looking at mass immigration from foreign countries into Northern cities, Grady—echoing sentiments of Washington and Jefferson on the same subject—urged the

South not to accept immigrants who might bring "heresies and discordant ideas." The South should only accept immigrants who come "to confirm and not to estrange, the simple faith in which we have been reared, and which we should transmit unsullied to our children."

In addition, Grady defended a feudal culture that had distinctions and a hierarchy. He charged that the North failed to understand this way of life; specifically the close relations it built between blacks and whites. The stability of a structured society was preferred over the levelling forces of socialism and urban culture. "The brotherhood of man is dissolving," he complained of late nineteenth-century America, "and people are huddling into masses." Even Donald Grady Davidson, Weaver's friend and booster, might have approved of the Henry Grady portrayed in *The Southern Tradition at Bay*.[19]

Weaver further credits liberals for tackling the region's race and education problems in a sensible and humane manner. *The Southern Tradition At Bay* discusses race with more candor (and more frequently) than other Weaver volumes. Race is rarely mentioned in *Ideas Have Consequences, Visions of Order* or even in many of Weaver's Southern essays. Some Southern views on race in this book fit the stereotypes which have plagued the region throughout its history. While Southern whites saw newly freed blacks as a people capable of producing their own musicians, poets, and orators, they did not see them as being fit to hold the franchise. In the South's defense, this was a mindset not at all different from the prevailing nineteenth-century American thought. Many Northern states, for instance, passed laws denying the franchise to their very small number of black citizens. Still, at this time, over 90 percent of the nation's blacks lived in the South. The problem could not be avoided. Some way of creating prosperity for the poor of both races had to be formulated. George Washington Cable called on whites to at least grant justice before the law to their black brethren. Without such rights, Southern politics might disintegrate into "solidarity, corruption [and] dishonesty."

Some liberals wanted to confront the race problem through public education. The idea of public education was never terribly popular with Richard Weaver; still he found the South's approach to be reasonable. The Reverend Edgar Murphy, an educator from Montgomery, Alabama, hoped that once Southern whites pulled themselves up from poverty, they might include blacks in a "program of general progress." Rev. Murphy's idea of public education was to promote "race sufficiency,'' where a race might produce its own "leaders and thinkers . . . scholars, artists and prophets." Attacking Marxists and other social engineers who sought to decimate all cultural distinctions (he also had in mind those who wanted involuntary desegregation), Weaver reminded readers that Rev. Murphy's ideas were the "views of one who studies the problem of a biracial community on the ground, and not in textbooks of revolutionaries."[20]

North Carolina's first post-Reconstruction governor, Charles Brantley Aycock was a prototype of the "first liberal." He made his case for public education by promising to preserve and uphold the heritage. Weaver understood that North Carolina was the one Southern state that was fertile ground for advancing public education. Lacking the aristocratic tradition of Virginia or South Carolina, the Tar Heel state tended more towards progressive notions than its neighbors. Aycock championed "universal book learning" but refused to surrender public schools to secularism. A strong defender of the older religiousness, Aycock, in a famous 1901 speech, announced to the world:

> Illiterate we have been, but ignorant never. Books we have not known, but men we have learned, and God we have sought to find out . . . nowhere within her [North Carolina's] borders a man known out of his township [is] ignorant enough to join with the fool in saying "There is no God."[21]

Aycock would only have public schools that taught the glories of the Southern past. In an audience that included President Theodore Roosevelt, he proclaimed that "[T]here is a South and a glorious South and we are not ashamed of what our fathers wrought in the days of '61 to '65." Traditions and distinctions were important to Aycock. He wanted an education built on developing individuality, inherited and distinctive traits, and the region's "own traditions" and "deep-rooted tendencies." Likewise, Rev. Murphy hoped the fallen Southern aristocracy would rise again to fulfill its traditional leadership role. Such formed Weaver's endorsement of this brand of Southern liberalism.

Liberals who failed were those either enamored of the money culture or frustrated by the tradition. The group of Southern governors who collaborated on a book, *Why the Solid South?* properly called on all patriotic Americans to understand the horrors of reconstruction. But the governors, Weaver noted, were right about this bleak era for the wrong reason. The book was written only to advise Northern businessmen that they could never bring their industries to a region that still hated the Yankee. In short, *Why the Solid South?* was written to end reconstruction and commence with—as Tom Watson shrewdly observed—the economic exploitation of the South by captains of industry. The South would liberate itself from political oppression only to welcome economic rule from afar. This economic style of liberalism was not worth pursuing.

Walter Hines Page, another Tar Heel liberal, railed against the feudal system, politicians, preachers, and the legacy of the aristocrats as impediments toward progress. Page liked the South. He knew the common man insisted on being "wrong in their own way, rather than right in another." He praised the region for rejecting the increasingly perverse New England world of "long haired men and short haired women." But the "unyielding stability of opinion" frustrated him more than the average liberal. Other liberals combined a method of what Weaver later termed "status and function." Traditions, pieties and mytholgies are important. Poverty and inertia had to be overcome with a program of progress that included poor whites and blacks (this is a necessary function) but the South needed to retain the ideal of the gentleman (this is status).

To save their culture, Southerners according to the "first liberals," needed to reclaim their past. Despite losing the war, the South still had to write its own history. The region needed to celebrate and reflect on the glories of its past—whether that meant the political achievement of Jefferson and Madison or the military legacy of Lee and Jackson. The South needed to preserve a society where an aristocracy of achievement is allowed to rejuvenate itself and assume its leadership position. And despite its postbellum condition of poverty and occupation, the region must not forsake the faiths of the older religiousness. Like Grady, Page wanted the South to become more open-minded, to develop an educational system, and produce goods for the nation and world. But to Weaver, Page was a liberal who failed to see redeeming values in the Southern tradition. He wanted progress, but he didn't realize that the legacy of the aristocrat was still important to his fellow Southerners.

One thing is certain: few Southern progressives of the postbellum age would be called "liberal" today. Grady's praise of the "social creeds of antebellum civilization" and his suspicion toward the ideology of the melting pot could only be an occasion for ridicule. The educational system envisioned by Aycock and Rev. Murphy would similarly be a cause for embarrassment. The emphasis on religion and tradition, the pride in the Southern past would be dismissed as hoplessly reactionary. In this sense, these liberals *were* reactionary. They knew the Radical Republicans planned a reconstruction that would obliterate every last vestige of Southern culture. The first liberals wanted no full-scale assault on the heritage. Like Weaver's Fugitive mentors, they "fled from nothing faster than the Brahmins of the Old South," identifying the "petrification" of the gentleman class as the region's greatest problem. But the first liberals did not see the past as an error so much as they sought to gently usher the region safely into a changing world.

Another theme of the postbellum charge is the attack on modernism. Since this term will come up throughout this study, we will define modernism as the rise of cities over the West's agrarian traditions. It also stands for planned economies, doctrines of "undefined" equality, the levelling of hierarchies, and the turning away from the idea of Christendom in favor of a wholly materialistic society. The postbellum attack on Leviathan called for Southerners to reject the business culture, secular democracy, and the march of the world's more powerful nations towards empire-building, a process that would result in "one-worldism" and the destruction of constitutional government.

Southern women, in particular, were members of the opposition party. Their story is one of the more interesting sections of *The Southern Tradition at Bay*. Looking at the impact of women writers, among them the novelist Augusta Jane Evans, diarists Mary Chesnut and Virginia Clay, Weaver declared that the South, both during and after the war, had become a "matriarchy." Influenced himself by the novels of Miss Evans, Weaver, writing in the early 1960s, still contended that women would have a more positive influence on society and the men who ran it if they did not have the franchise. In other words, they would have a civilizing effect on their men. As voters (and eventually, politicians), they only competed with men. The wholly positive feminine influence would be lost.

When the war ended, Southern women took over, teaching their children a proper history of the conflict, encouraging their downtrodden husbands and embarking on an ambitious monument-building effort. Jefferson Davis was so moved by their wartime efforts that he dedicated his two-volume memoirs to all Southern women. Weaver even speculated that if Southern ladies were in charge of the war effort, then Robert E. Lee would indeed have escaped to the mountains to fight for another twenty years (as he once vowed) rather than surrendering at Appomattox.[22]

Why were Southern women so feisty? Weaver explains it as a thumping rejection of the business culture. Southern women knew what they liked in a man. And they sure didn't care for the coming of a bourgeois age. The Confederate soldier represented a romantic ideal. The ladies preferred a man who displayed characteristics of "bravery, generosity, personal aplomb and a gift for large talk." He was part of an equally romantic society that "satisfied primary longings." The war itself soon became a "business transaction." And the new age it ushered in was represented by "tired and unromantic businessmen." The era of chivalry was being replaced by the rise of an equally "unromantic middle class" with those uninspiring attributes being "thrift, sobriety, patience and the kind of plodding industry which creates bourgeois security."[23]

Southern women made the case that a business culture (or an industrial society) destroyed the spirit of romance. There was no room for daring, risk-taking individuals. All would melt into the new urban masses. As such, there was no longer a place for the gentleman or the lady. Men and women from now on would be in a ceaseless competition for whatever prizes the material world offered.

The business world of a complacent middle-class was bad enough. Even more troubling for many postbellum thinkers was the rise of secular democracy. In the tradition of the older religiousness, Southern theologians urged their followers to reject a new secular democracy in motion all across the land. Bledsoe singled out the French Revolution for introducing heresies that made "man as the measure of all things." Rev. Robert Dabney blasted secular democracy for ignoring man's evil instincts, arguing instead that religion was needed to influence democracy.

Moreover, Southern politicians, lawyers, and journalists, in a more prosaic manner, all claimed the South's defeat ruined the idea of a "conservative Western democracy" in the United States and perhaps the entire world. Volumes by Jefferson Davis, Alexander Stephens, and others duly documented the constitutional right of secession. Davis, for instance, noted earlier secession movements in New England. The South was no different and no less in the right. Unreconstructed to the end, Davis also urged Southerners to continue to fight the good fight for constitutional government.

Stephens, on the other hand, was less sanguine. He agreed that the war and reconstruction had wrecked the Constitution, but he also stated that the South was a victim of global trends. The entire world was marching towards "emperor worship." Only when this powerful and suffocating force prevailed worldwide, would the globe's citizens then see the rightness of the Southern cause. Inspired by the South's unsuccessful rebellion, the world might then throw off the shackles of one-world government.

Stephens, of course, was proved prophetic (at least about the tendencies towards empire) and Weaver seconds the former vice president's claim that the South was victim of ominous nineteenth-century ideologies. Science and rationalism were in the saddle; so was empire-building. The mid-nineteenth-century West was marching down the road towards industrialism and the construction of powerful centralized governments. Overseas expansion fit in nicely with these revolutionizing developments. Even the United States, with the Spanish-American War (which Southerners eagerly supported) had its first fling with overseas imperialism.

Weaver generally disliked arguments made by politicians and lawyers. They made correct legal points, but that was hardly enough; there was not the necessary metaphysical argument. Again, the South was "right without knowing the grounds of its rightness." Fortunately, Weaver is here to show us the way. The Southern apologists got it right when they defended the South's nonmaterialistic sentiments. Most of them preferred the "unbought grace of life" to the material gains that seemed to be the sole purpose of the business culture. Echoing Jefferson and anticipating Weaver's Vanderbilt mentors, the apologists praised the old agrarian culture. Albert Taylor Bledsoe called farming "the most innocent vocation and . . . the best training in virtue." Edward Pollard saw an agrarian people as "happy, tolerant, reverent," while inhabitants of urban cultures were an unstable and unhappy people: "Sensations, excitements on slight cause, fits of fickle admiration, manias in society and fashion, a regard for magnitude, display and exaggeration, all are indications of a superficial and restless civilization." Thomas Dixon added that Southerners were "medieval, old fashioned . . . busy raising children rather than making money."

The apologists also preferred a society built upon a conservative constitution rather than pleasant-sounding abstractions. Likewise, they rejeced the idea of the United States as "a universal nation" (as our present-day boosters like to define America). Instead they defended the particularisms of their own people and culture. The Kentucky journalist Henry Watterson championed provincialism, asking with what became an often-repeated battle-cry: "What good is it to gain the world if I lose my soul?" as the United States embarked on its own era of empire-building abroad. Weaver also found this aspect of the apology both correct and effective. It harkened to the permanent, concrete things that breathe life into civilizations. The case for particularisms of a people and against universalism was summed up in one fiery passage from the most unreconstructed of the apologists. In *The Leopard's Spots*, a Thomas Dixon character makes this political stemwinder:

> I am in a sense narrow and provincial. I love mine own people. Their past is mine, their future is a divine trust. I hate the dishwater of modern world citizenship. A shallow cosmopolitanism is the mask of death for the individual. It is the froth of civilization, as crime is its dregs. The true citizen of the world loves his country.[24]

Despite the apologists' overall failure in their philosophical arguments, Weaver held great hope in the legacy left by these mostly forgotten writers. In the early 1960s, he wrote an epilogue to *The Southern Tradition at Bay* which was included in the published text. We are fortunate to have it; the section contains some of the most moving, most powerful passages of his career. It is as complete a summary of Weaver's philosophy that we have. Why did Weaver see great hope for the legacy of the Southern tradition? It was, after all, "at bay," not totally defeated.

Specifically, there was the world's continued fascination with the Old South. Weaver may have been thinking of several factors. The 1930s saw great interest in the Old South through the popular culture; Margaret Mitchell's *Gone With The Wind* became both the most popular novel and motion picture of all time. Popular culture, mediocre as it may be, is still a barometer of an age. More to the point was the Southern literary renaissance of the 1930s, with William Faulkner, Thomas Wolfe, John Crowe Ransom, Allen Tate, Caroline Gordon, Donald Davidson, and Robert Penn Warren, among others, all producing the South's first great contributions to world literature. The Fugitive movement would evolve into the Agrarian movement, and the publication of *I'll Take My Stand* announced to the nation that at least some Southerners were willing to defend their birthright. The enduring legacy of the Old South portrayed a region that represented an antidote to state worship—whether that was the dreary collectivism gathering strength in the United States or the mad rush towards the complete state as practiced by fascists and communists in Europe.[25] Men will learn someday "to live strenuously or romantically," Weaver boldly proclaims in the epilogue. When they return to those more heroic instincts, modern man will also be able to overthrow the "social security welfare state" that reduces him to a mere economic unit. If this can't be done, then severe consequences await us.

> We are being narrowed down to one nation, one world, in which nobody can move an elbow without jostling those in the farthest corner; and the danger of friction is so great that liberty of opposition must be decreased, channeled, and there must stand ready a supreme authority ready to strike down any menace to peace, to its peace, to the status quo. The emperor or dictator, of completely pervasive authority, backed by an oligarchy of scientist—that is the situation into which forces are hurrying us. The state becomes a monolith, rigid with fear that it has lost control of its destiny. We all stand today at Appomattox, and we are surrendering to a world which this hypostatized science has made in our despite.[26]

As Tom Landess notes, each Weaver book is "different in concept and focus." *The Southern Tradition at Bay* is Weaver's most ambitious effort. No other Weaver effort is as large (nearly 400 pages) or as lively, with such a diverse picture of the South, ranging from books that were sentimental (the novels of Thomas Nelson Page) to tragic (here one thinks of Richard Taylor's commentary on the war) to comical (especially the satirical novels of Opie Read). Since the end of the Middle Ages, Weaver saw very little good happening in the destiny of the West. The Old South, despite its faults, carried the "mandate of civilization" and is worthy of receiving fair play in history.

Furthermore, the enormous scholarship that distinguishes *The Southern Tradition at Bay* alone makes it a daunting achievement. Indeed, the book is a great historical document, a thorough study of the postbellum South and as such, an indispensable history of a tragic era in American civilization. Like its epilogue, much of *The Southern Tradition at Bay* is a very moving book: The story of a defeated people coming to grips with a strange, hostile world, while at the same time clinging to the faiths of their fathers. In this respect, the book can also be read as an important—and highly underrated—tragedy in American literature.

The Southern Tradition at Bay shaped Weaver's own philosophy. In succeeding books, he was able to hone and sharpen themes first introduced here. The comparisons between agrarian and urban culture, for instance, would become more pronounced as would criticism of "economic democracy," and mass education. Weaver was not finished with his study of Southern culture; he would continue to compare favorably its particularisms to the larger condition of the Western world. Inspired by the revolt of his ancestors, and with his worldview more fully formed, Richard Weaver was ready to launch his own revolt against a decadent age.

3

Man in Megalopolis:
Ideas Have Consequences

Now we fast forward a good four decades from the last days of the Old South in the twentieth early century to a Western world left bleeding by the total warfare of World War II. In 1945, Richard Weaver was an assistant professor in the University of Chicago's English Department, the author of only a handful of published essays and reviews. World War II, the abandonment of Finland, and the sellout of the rest of Eastern Europe at Yalta all inspired the beginnings of *Ideas Have Consequences*. For Weaver, the entire war effort suddenly seemed less noble and worthwhile. "I recall sitting in&My office in Ingleside Hall at the University of Chicago one Fall morning in 1945 and wondering whether it would not be possible to deduce, from fundamental causes, the fallacies of modern life and thinking that had produced this holocaust and would ensure others," he wrote a decade later. "I jotted down a series of chapter headings and this was the inception of . . . *Ideas Have Consequences*."[1]

The book also had its genesis in conversations with Cleanth Brooks and W.T. Couch. By the mid-1940s Brooks had established himself as one of the nation's leading literary critics. Formerly a professor at Louisiana State University, Brooks, on the strength of his criticism (including such books as *The Well Wrought Urn*) and his co-editorship, along with Robert Penn Warren of *The Southern Review*, had been aggressively recruited by several prestigious Northern universities. The administration at Baton Rouge made no great effort to keep this rising literary star, so Brooks soon found a permanent home at Yale University. But while at LSU, Brooks had also been a director for Weaver's dissertation and the two continued their friendship. Couch, formerly director of the University of North Carolina Press, was now editor of the University Press at Chicago. Both Brooks and Couch told Weaver that books on the South had only a limited appeal among publishers and the reading public: Why not instead, write a critique of modern life in general? Weaver's new home in Chicago gave him a useful perspective on the dominant urban culture of postwar America. And so a new book was started in 1945 and finished two years later. Weaver had no problem finding a publisher for this project. While at UNC, Couch was part of the committee that rejected *The Southern Tradition at Bay*. Accepting *Ideas* may have been Couch's way of making up for that earlier error.[2]

Chivalry was a key element of the Southern tradition. It was an ideal that also inspired the writing of *Ideas Have Consequences*. Appalled by the total warfare of World War II, Weaver turned to the "bygone ideal of chivalry" as a way of keeping inevitable warfare "within civilization." The book does contain a defense of chivalry. But *Ideas Have Consequences* mostly is a withering assault on urban culture, using the rise of the masses as a metaphor for the fall of civilization.

In *Ideas,* Weaver asserts that twentieth-century man is wallowing in the abyss of confusion and anarchy, and shows how he might pull himself up from that abyss and live, once again, in civilized communities. *Ideas* begins modestly enough: "This is another book on the dissolution of the West." What follows is a 189–page jeremiad, one of the first great philosophical tracts of the post-World War II era. Right from the beginnning, the reader notes a language that is urgent, angry, and apocalyptic. What George Nash called "the rending of Christendom" inspired the rhetoric of *Ideas Have Consequences*. Indeed, nearly fifty years after its publication, the book has lost none of its capacity to sting, provoke, and enlighten the reader. Consider these observations as Weaver contemplates a Western world sent reeling by global warfare:

> Surely we are justified in saying of our time: If you seek the monument of folly, look about you. In our own day, we have seen cities obliterated, and ancient faiths stricken. We may well ask, in the words of Matthew, whether we are not faced with "great tribulation, such as was not since the beginning of the world." We have

for many years moved with a brash confidence that man had achieved a position of independence which rendered the ancient restraints needless. Now, in the first half of the twentieth century, at the height of modern progress, we behold unprecedented outbreaks of hatred and violence. We have seen whole nations desolated by war and turned into penal camps by their conquerers; we find half of mankind looking upon the other half as criminal.[3]

This paragraph captured the mood of the immediate postwar years, when many intellectuals, despondent over the discovery of the Holocaust, the use of nuclear weapons and the heightening Cold War between the West and the Soviet Union, feared even greater catastrophies looming on the horizon. If it wasn't total war that would destroy us, then the realization of the total state might do the job. As such, there is this unforgettable description of twentieth-century man, a creature cut off from his past, lost in megalopolis. Instead of being liberated by modern progress, he has:

the look of the hunted. He senses that we have lost our grip upon reality. This, in turn produces disintegration and disintegration leaves impossible that kind of reasonable prediction by which men, in eras of sanity, are able to order their lives. And the fear accompanying it unlooses the great disorganizing force of hatred, so that states are threatened and war ensues. Few men today feel certain that war will not wipe out their children's inheritance; and even if this evil is held in abeyance, the individual does not rest easy, for he knows that the Juggernaut technology may twist or destroy the patterns of life he has made for himself.[4]

In *The Southern Tradition at Bay,* we are introduced to Weaver's fondness for the culture of the Middle Ages. So it follows that in Weaver's view the end of the Middle Ages set Western man down the road to barbarism. For Weaver, modern decadence had its roots in the fourteenth century with the rise of nominalism as set forth by William of Occam. To modern readers, even college-educated ones, this is an obscure figure. So what was wrong with this new philosophy? Simply put, Western man gave up his belief in a Higher Being, instead becoming "his own priest and ethics professor." "The practical result of nominalist philosophy," Weaver declared, "is to banish the reality which is perceived by the intellect and to posit as reality that which is perceived by the senses." Thus the road to decadence.

The rise of nominalism precipitated the fall of Christendom, even though Weaver, still in his agnostic state, doesn't come out and say it that bluntly. Still, the downhill slide began with Western man abandoning the idea of original sin. Without original sin as his guide, modern man denied even the existence of evil. Believing in his own superiority, he now saw nature as a force to conquer. Thus science became the great secular religion. Science could not only overcome the limitations set up by nature, it could lead man to a life of ease and comfort. No longer would man have to earn his daily bread by the sweat of his brow.

Science was followed by the new religion of deism. Deism had failed in the American South (Thomas Jefferson had introduced it in his University of Virginia, but in time that ideology was rejected). However, it triumphed throughout much of the West. Deism was a "humanistic" religion, which "makes God the outcome of a rational reading of nature." Deism was a religion that also allowed man to mold God in his own image. It was convenient, then, for man to create a God that only "loves us all," in effect, freeing man to live a life of sin without fear of retribution. In short, man created what John Crowe Ransom called a "God without thunder."

The image of God and man had changed dramatically. God was a benevolent force. Man was now a consuming animal. Away went the ancient struggle between good and evil. In came the doctrine of survival of the fittest—a direct antitheses of the Middle Ages and Old South where the knight was obliged to defend the helpless. Rationalism preached the goodness of man. Science showed him how nature could be conquered. Materialism turned man's quest into not one of justice, but of wealth and consumption. With accumulation of material goods now the main goal of life, the flight from the country to the city commenced. In the context of Weaver's criticism of modern life, this is the most urgent consequence of the "evil decision."

The portrait of modern man in *Ideas Have Consequences*, then, is of man in megalopolis. By megalopolis, Weaver does not only mean the cities, but the entire metropolitan area, including the vast suburbs, where a complacent middle class holds sway. *Ideas Have Consequences* is similar in both its theme and structure to Ortega y Gasset's more famous *The Revolt of the Masses*. Both men viewed the triumph of an urban culture with great trepidation. What Ortega y Gasset called the "minority" fit for leadership roles, Weaver would term a "hierarchy." But now the civilizing forces of distinctions which allowed each man to find his place of value in society has been destroyed.

Man is viewed throughout the book as wholly ignoble and unheroic. Weaver thought modern man was all-too-corruptible; he also saw him as a tragic figure. Modern man, Weaver noticed, takes no pleasure from his work. He is no longer a craftsman in the medieval sense of the word, but a worker who has neither independence or any real economic power. Told he has more power than his agrarian ancestors, his economic destiny is in fact in the hands of industrialists, multinational corporations, and monopolies, all seeing modern men (and women) as forms of cheap labor. Economic independence, Weaver declared, is "too expensive." Personal integrity is a "prohibitive luxury." While his ancestors enjoyed a "sense of abundance" through their work from the land, modern man in his office or factory suffers from a "sense of scarcity." Often, he resents even the idea of work as he has been told by his demagogic masters that a life of ease and comfort is now a birthright.

While pointing out this modern-day form of servitude, Weaver also took memorable swipes against urban culture. *Ideas Have Consequences* quickly became famous for its wide-ranging broadsides against popular culture: tabloid newspapers, radio, movies, jazz music; not to mention attacks on such modern-day sacred cows as economic democracy, "undefined equality," and mass education. Weaver isn't as colorful as Andrew Lytle, who urged us to chuck the radio and take the bow and fiddle down from the wall, but he agreed with Lytle that modern culture was a highly corrupting force. Weaver called it "The Great Stereopticon," the world of the mass media which gives us a false and extremely negative (as opposed to honest) view of both man's nature and history itself. There was also rampant egotism in more traditional mediums—literature and painting—which now celebrated the artist's vanity and spontaneity. Works of art were once true to history. Their treatment of tragedy and man's heroic qualities created the mythologies that sustained civilizations throughout the generations. The egotism of modern art has grounded this process to a halt. To Weaver, egotism in art represented "a heresy about man's destiny," even though "its absence of discipline and form is usually grouped with signs of progress."

Weaver was equally critical of nineteenth- and twentieth-century-style democracy. Specifically, he had no use for a democracy centered only around economic rhetoric. Willmoore Kendall has noted that Weaver, when addressing the nation's problems, was not the type to care much about the size of the Gross National Product. In short, if democracy means "who gets what," then Weaver would denounce it.

However, if it asks deeper, more Socratic questions, such as what does it mean to be a free man living in a free society, then Weaver would find redeemable qualities in a modern democracy. Richard Weaver was a young man when he wrote this book, so we can excuse some youthful idealism.[5]

On culture, Weaver reserved his greatest ire for the rise in popularity of jazz music. Such criticim is controversial—it even sounds prudish to us jaded moderns—only in that jazz has long been considered a rather benign form of culture, an innocent piece of Americana, conjuring up images of musicians playing for tourists on Bourbon Street in New Orleans. But for Weaver, the rise of jazz represented nothing less than the ransacking of the civilized world by "society's fifth column—the barbarians inside the gates."

The emergence of jazz, according to Weaver, dramatized a great global sickness. He describes its baneful influence with the book's characteristically apocalyptic language. Consider these examples: "Something in the Negro's spontaneous manifestation of feeling linked up with Western man's declining faith in the value of his culture." Or the contention that jazz illustrates "our age's deep-seated predilication for barbarism," and the charge that its popularity also "indicates some vast extent of inward ravage, so that there were no real barriers against the disintegration it represents."[6]

Jazz also signified all that was wrong with modern art. It found an audience among the bored, passive masses "impatient for titillation." Jazz also represented another form of "contempt for labor." Because it appealed to the senses, jazz mocked form and ritual, piety and sacrifice. Jazz, too, presented a false view of life. True, it was hailed as the "music of freedom," but since it was all spontaneous, it also celebrated man's barbaric impulses and only was a case of "freedom from" forms and restraints. Jazz was music for a particularly decadent age:

By dissolving forms, it has left man free to move without reference, expressing dithyrambically whatever surges up from below. It is the music not of dreams . . . but of drunkenness. . . . Here, indeed, is a music to go with empiricism, and it is only natural that the chief devotees of jazz should be the primitive, the young and those persons, fairly numerous, who take pleasure in the thought of bringing down our civilization. The fact that the subjects of jazz, in so far as it may be said to have subjects, are grossly sexual or farcical—subjects of love without aesthetic distance and subjects of comedy without law of proportion—shows how the soul of modern man craves orgiastic disorder. And it is admitted that what man expresses in music dear to him he will most certainly express in his social practices.[7]

For an example of undefined equality gone haywire, Weaver examines modern man's treatment of the fairer sex. No doubt Weaver would be appalled by politicians and editorialists making solemn remarks about "our fighting men and women." But again, he foresaw all this during the war years, predicting the day when women "would be bombed in a foxhole" along with her male counterpart (with whom she now enjoyed full equality). As with the rise of jazz, modern man's treatment of women was, for Weaver, another striking example of twentieth-century barbarism. We are, in effect, depriving women of their "queenliness" by deciding femininity itself is inferior to the glories of manhood. Thus the attempt to "masculinize" women.

Undefined equality, to Weaver, was destructive because it creates endless competition, jealousies, and resentments between the sexes—which for twentieth-century America was most strikingly carried out in the economic arena. Because it denies the existence of distinctions among individuals, equality also destroys a sense of fraternity. The "battle of the sexes," first recognized by popular culture in the 1970s, initially seemed harmless enough, a plaything for the upper-middle classes. But needless competition between the sexes had, in time, their own consequences: High divorce rates, the proliferation of one-parent families, two generations (and counting) of boys without fathers and the corresponding astronomical rise in juvenile crime—not shoplifting or truancy, but murder, rape, and robbery.

Women in the workforce was also a consequence of industrialism and the war economy of the 1940s, phenomena the Old Right generally despised. The "global economy" of the post-World War II years has only exacerbated the situation. Foreign competition, mainly from cheap labor in Third World nations has, over the past two decades, flattened American wages, ending the era of the father as a family's sole breadwinner, thus forcing more women out of the home and into the working world. Again, such ominous trends were anticipated in this most prophetic of all Weaver volumes.

Weaver is correct in noting that women employees have been exploited, but Andrew Lytle said it better when he claimed that modern women originally went to work out of boredom. When an agrarian culture reigned, women had plenty of tasks to keep them busy. While their men worked in the fields, women cooked meals, preserved the milk and butter, and sewed clothes. At lunchtime, (which was "supper" back then), the family gathered for a large, sumptuous meal.

When industrialism destroyed the agrarian order, men left the farm for less responsible work and women found their own tasks replaced by technology. With nothing else to do, women left the farm themselves and entered the workforce as another form of "manpower."[8]

Today, women often work out of necessity. Either way, we are paying a terrible price for this loss of economic independence. Here is Weaver's pithy explanation and description of a catastrophe not so evident in 1948, but all too familiar to our fractured society:

> With her superior closeness to nature, her intuitive realism, unfailing ability to detect the sophistry in mere intellectuality, how was she ever cozened into the mistake of going modern? Perhaps it was the decay of chivalry in men that proved too much. After the gentleman went, the lady had to go, too. No longer protected, the woman now has her career, in which she makes a drab pilgrimage from two-room apartment to job to divorce court.[9]

To sum up urban man's condition in a single phrase, Weaver would assert that barbarians were in the saddle, and twentieth-century man had become a spoiled child. While his ancestors spilt their blood to settle the frontier and build a life free from bureaucracy, Western man now expects a life of "entitlements" from the cradle to the grave. The strenuous life has become impossible to attain; anyway, people don't want it. To make matters worse, the consequences of radical egalitarianism were wide-scale resentments, which, as Weaver cites Richard Hertz, "may well prove [to be] the dynamite which will finally wreck Western society."[10]

Submerged into the masses, man in megalopolis was now at the mercy of political demagogues. In fact, Weaver was so pessimistic about the future of economic democracy that he saw the demagogue as the *only* political "leader" who would emerge from the wreckage of the times. When the life of ease and comfort failed to materialize, the demagogue offered an array of scapegoats—Weaver listed the fallen aristocracy, intellectuals, millionaires, members of racial minorities, "Southern Bourbons," captains of industry—to blame for modern man's supposedly impoverished material condition (Weaver was indiscriminate in drawing up this list; its members have been targeted by demagogues on all sides of the political spectrum). The triumph of fascism in Europe was certainly on Weaver's mind, but he also felt the surviving Western democracies were not immune from the raging viruses of smouldering resentments. Blaming "economic royalists" smacks of

Franklin Roosevelt's worst excesses. A Southern patriot, Weaver, nonetheless, was unhappy with the rise of Huey Long. In fact, Weaver never stopped mourning the fall of the gentleman and the rise of his "white trash" demagogic successor. Moreover, living in the city allowed Weaver to witness the workings of big-city machine politics, which specializing in patronage, bribe taking, and ballot fixing, offered no shortage of glittering material promises.

Ideas Have Consequences is a riveting jeremiad against modern life, but its underlying message is also the stuff of tragedy, namely, that there comes a time when decadence is so great, so ingrained in a society that it becomes impossible for that civilization to pull itself out of the abyss. Weaver asked stern questions of his fellow citizens; he claimed "nothing less than a second coming" in the political culture of the West was needed to arrest modern decline. In the late 1940s, Weaver was not sanguine about the future. He didn't give up hope; as M.E. Bradford has noted, Weaver was too much the gentleman to be terminally pessimistic. However, with this book, Weaver meant to grab the reader by the throat—and he succeeded brilliantly. In this devastating critique, there is no finer passage summing up the fallen state of the spoiled child.

> The Stereopticon has shielded him from the sight of the abyss, [so] that he conceives the world to be a fairly simple machine, which . . . can be made to go. And going, it turns out comforts and whatever satisfactions his demagogic leaders have told him he is entitled to. But mysteries are always intruding, so that even the best-designed machine has been unable to effect a continuous operation. No less than his ancestors, he finds himself up against toil and trouble. Since this was not nominated in the bond, he suspects evildoers and takes the childish course of blaming individuals for things inseparable from the human condition. The truth is that he has never brought to see what it is to be a man. That man is the product of discipline of forging, that he really owes thanks for the pulling and tugging that enable him to grow—this concept left the manuals of education with the advent of Romanticism. This citizen is now the child of indulgent parents who pamper his appetites and inflate his egotism until he is unfitted for struggle of any kind.[11]

Rural Man/Urban Man

Weaver did not dislike the urban man. A great humanist, he understood the hardships and agony modern man felt by living in cities "where all the vices of urban and industrial society break forth in a kind of evil flower." He understood the "hunger" modern man felt from being cut off from any real and viable tradition or the disillusionment brought on by whiling away his time at menial tasks. When urban man is materially successful, he becomes so through a world of abstractions, dealing in stocks and bonds and paper exchanges. In such an atmosphere, man loses sight of the "mysteries of creation." A stock that goes up one day, falls the next. None of it is very real. Like most traditionalists, Weaver disliked the world of unfettered, Wall Street-style capitalism.[12]

And so, another great theme that runs through the book is the comparison between urban man and rural man; a comparison, that not surprisingly results in another rousing defense of agrarian life. In *The Southern Tradition at Bay,* the hero was the landed gentleman, but the hero of *Ideas Have Consequences* is the yeoman farmer. His virtues are numerous: As someone who has worked on the land and dealt in real commodities like wheat, corn, tobacco and livestock, the rural man constantly contemplated the same mysteries of nature that urban man has ignored. Like the workers who built the cathedrals of Catholic Europe, the rural man's work is guided by ideals. Traditions live longer in rural communities. People there have longer memories. For rural people, "what their grandfathers did is real to them." Rural man, then, is free of the "hysterical optimism" which denies the existence of tragedy and is the great siren song of the Stereopticon. He is calm in times of crisis, less agitated and fretful than his urban counterpart. As such, the rural man, whether the gentleman or the yeoman farmer, is fit for the leadership role. Weaver would have preferred the gentleman, but either way, the rural man is the backbone of a pious social order. Through his example Weaver is especially trying to restore the sanctity (and joy) of work itself as a goal higher than material gain.

For a fuller portrait of the ideal American citizen, Weaver reached back to mid-nineteenth-century America to recall the dignified, freedom-loving man of the soil. Weaver's inspired portrait of the Vermont farmer invites comparison to Donald Davidson's famous essay "Still Rebels, Still Yankees" in which the Tennessean celebrates the uncompromisng individualism of both the Vermont farmer, "Brother Jonathan" and his South Georgia counterpart dubbed "Cousin Roderick." Perhaps, like Davidson, Weaver was gently trying to explain how the Civil War—by heralding the new age of industrialism, the all-powerful centralized state and mass culture—eventually destroyed not only the agrarian South, but also the comparable pastoral New England civilization.

Whatever the case, Weaver's Vermont farmer represents the Jeffersonian ideal. He is a man who plows his own land, but who is also well-integrated into his community, a man "with enough character to say No"—presumably, to a Leviathan State that would seek to control him:

> Let us look . . . at preindustrial America. The feature of that society which contrasts most strongly with our own was the distribution of centers of influence and authority. We might take as a single instance a Vermont farmer of the 1850s, certainly not one to give himself airs, yet a vessel of some responsibility and, to that extent, an aristocrat by calling. He has been properly admired for his independence, by which is meant not isolation from community . . . but opportunity and disposition to decide for himself according to a rational and enduring code of values. His acres may have been rocky, but he appraised his situation and assumed direction. He rose early because the relationship between effort and reward was clear to him. There was a rhythm to his task which humanized it; each day bringing a certain round of duties, and the seasons themselves imposing a larger pattern, as when haying time arrived. At the end of the day, he might remain up until nine o'clock with the weekly newspaper, not flying through comics and sporting news but reading its political disquisitions to weigh and consider as carefully as Bacon could have desired. He observed the Fourth of July, Thanksgiving and Christmas with some recollection of what they signified. He remained poor, but he was not unmanned; he had enough character to say No.[13]

There are more examples, one of which is perhaps sentimental, but taken seriously by the author. Weaver tells the story of an Oklahoma dirt farmer who, upon hearing of America's entry into World War II, leaves his home for the West Coast to work in a defense factory. The farmer is illiterate; each week he receives a small piece of paper whose contents he cannot read. After compiling a number of such papers, he asks his wife what they signify. He is dumbfounded when she tells him they are paychecks. The dirt farmer assumed in times of crisis "everyone pitches in." Piety, in this case, demands each man serve his country—and one need not be paid for doing so. Even while discussing the debilitating effects of the Stereopticon, Weaver manages to trumpet the virtues of rural man. He cites a Bureau of Agriculture economic study which shows that while city people preferred radio comedy and variety shows, rural listeners opted for more serious programming: religious sermons, news and market reports, and farm news. If we must have the Stereopticon, such broadcasting will suffice.

The world of the Vermont farmer forms the foundation of Weaver's steps to get modern man out of his rut, to, in effect, "de-mass the masses." The final three chapters extol the virtues of private property and piety; one chapter, "The Power of the Word" urges a return to the reverence (that is, honesty) in the spoken and written word. Private property and piety go hand-in-hand. Russell Kirk saw some weaknesses in Weaver's thesis, noting that there is no such thing as *complete* private property (after all, we pay property taxes on our land). But this was a subject (as it was to Kirk) that was close to Weaver's life and heritage. After escaping Chicago, Weaver plowed his own patch of land in Weaverville each summer. As noted earlier, he also planned on returning to the land once his teaching career in the big city ended. "The Last Metaphysical Right" defended private property as a vehicle of responsibility, an antidote to both economic socialism and rampant materialism.[14]

For starters, private property gives us protection from the ominipotent state, providing us with "entrenchment against pagan statism" and assumes that "not all shall be dependent on the state." Free from the centralized state, man's sense of responsibility turns him to the belief in a Higher Authority. The rural man's responsibility toward his property cultivates a strong sense of piety. When a bumper crop comes in, farmers and their families praise the goodness of God for their good fortune.[15]

Private property also provides training in virtue. Such responsibilities force a man to "express his true personal nature," leading to an ideal condition when a man is now "only as good as his work." Private property, Weaver contended, was a vehicle for breaking down the socialism of the "global economy." Weaver cherished the Old Republic, when certain products, whether they be New England ships, Pennsylvania iron, or Virginia tobacco, conjured up images of quality and pride in workmanship. But something strange was happening in this new economic order. If Weaver disliked unrestrained capitalism (the markets are not always "moral" as many conservatives have ruefully learned), he also saw no use for multinational corporations and monopolies. To Weaver, the names these new global merchants use for their companies, "General," "Standard," and "International" symbolized the passing of an era. They stood as a "mark of adulteration" where "no man may be responsible." Such products also represented an economic order where regional cultures and old ways of doing things were considered obsolete. Pennsylvania iron or Virginia tobacco, on the other hand, were things a man could believe in. They signified allegiance to a state or community—which, as we have noted, was a defining characteristic of early America. Such products created a sense of honor, guiding us back to the days when men were craftsmen, not mere workers.

Private property, finally, provides an antidote to materialism. Throughout the book Weaver mercilessly lays waste to the grand claims of modern progress. Mainly he attacks the vain idea that the present date in history—whether it is 1947 or 1997—represents the highest point of material and human progress in all recorded history. Thus we are free to agree with Henry Ford that "all history is bunk" while continuing newer and more bizarre experiments in social engineering.

Weaver's most pointed rebuke to the idea of progress comes with the example of housing. In older days, a man simply built a house with his own hands (and sometimes, with workers to assist him). The house itself was a classic instance of private property: No bank had domain over it. The building of a house was an honorable, sacred task, done with great selflessness. Houses were built "with an eye toward the third generation." That is, they were built more for the man's children and grandchildren than for his own comfort. Drive through the countryside in New England or the South, Weaver tells us. There in the quiet villages and towns one can still see houses that reflect not only honesty, but grace and form. The builder, also, succeeded in his goal. The houses still stand, habitable and sturdy, a century and a half after being built. All this is a pleasing alternative to the modern method of housing. There the modern builder constructs housing for the "anonymous buyer" with an eye only on the profit margin. The buyer is glad to own something, but he is also stuck with a long mortgage which circumstances may someday prevent him from paying. Furthermore, the houses are of poor quality. Far from being usable to the buyer's children and grandchildren (who will be lucky to even go through the same mortgage process), these houses, after twenty years or so, are falling apart.

Private property, piety, and honest rhetoric. These three steps might seem like a thin reed to some, but one gets the feeling they were only opening shots in a long battle. All throughout *Ideas Have Consequences*—and in other books—the virtues of rural man are continuously cited in the face of enormous economic and sociological change. But mostly Weaver celebrated the timelessness of a rural culture; Donald Davidson, making his own mid-twentieth-century defense of agrarianism, eloquently complemented Weaver's own similiar philosophy.

There is no other really human basis upon which to build a social order unless we return . . . to some kind of simple pastoral life. But the agrarian life is neither a going back nor a going forward, it has nothing to do with the illusion of progress or decadence, it knows nothing of the straight line. Life is a timeless cycle, not a line, and the agrarian life establishes man within that natural cycle where he belongs. This is the place to build whatever you may want to build. Those who have argued the contrary are now seeing what it costs to support an industrial order, when it becomes the order of life; when indeed it gives orders, as it must, not only in the factory and office, but everywhere.[16]

The Weaver Revolution

Critics noted shortcomings in *Ideas Have Consequences*. There was, for example, little discussion of religion. The decline of the West was due, in part, to a lack of faith in a "higher authority," but Weaver does not come out and say the fall was caused by the collapse of Christendom. A reviewer in *Commonweal* noticed that when Weaver seemed to be prescribing a remedy based on Catholicism, the author "stopped dead in his tracks" as if he knew such a cure was necessary.[17]

Likewise, some readers objected to Weaver's disdain for the middle class. In our time, the middle class has stood for what stability that exists in American life, representing moral decency, family life, economic prosperity, and security. Both political parties strive mightily to curry favor with middle-class voters, upholding such values as the very foundations of American civilization. But as Weaver points out, the welfare state exists mostly for the benefit of a complacent middle class. He had little hope for a people so dependent on the Leviathan state. Throughout the 1950s, Weaver would continue this critique. Such criticism was part of his dislike for the modern-day welfare state, but also an example of Weaver's ever-present candor. One can't expect to go far by attacking proper bourgeois civilization, especially when those attacks came from the Right. Less convincing was Weaver's criticism of the entrepreneur. In our urban/industrial society, with many citizens at the mercy of the state, the entrepreneur represents the risk-taking spirit that characterized the Old Republic.

Upon its publication, *Ideas Have Consequences* caused an immediate uproar in the intellectual community and gained a fame that completely surprised its author. No other book by Weaver was reviewed more widely or discussed so heatedly. Over 100 reviews of the book appeared, covering a vast spectrum from the far Left (Communist party papers in the U.S. even took their shot at *Ideas*) to praise from Weaver's Agrarian mentors. The rending of economic democracy, mass education, undefined equality, plus the support of an old-fashioned hierarchy all earned Weaver the ire of liberal critics.

Two essays in *Antioch Review* were especially hostile. George Geiger denounced Weaver as a "pompous fraud" and termed *Ideas* an "evil book." Geiger claimed modern man could solve his problems "by a critical and reflective intelligence" or he can "run away from his problems by questing for certainty and postulating a fairyland of absolute essences. It is what Mr. Weaver does." Herbert J. Muller called Weaver's agrarian program for restoration "hopelessly quixotic." Both science and industrialism are here to stay. Why bother fighting them? W.E. Garrison, writing in the *Christian Century*, concurred, blasting Weaver as a "propagandist for a return to the medieval papacy."[18]

But that criticism was balanced by strong praise from a loosely defined group of conservatives and traditionalists. The 1959 paperback edition featured recommendations by John Crowe Ransom, Paul Tillich, and Reinhold Niebuhr. Tillich noted that the book will "shock" adding with admiration that "philosophical shock is the beginning of wisdom." W.A. Orton praised *Ideas* as "one of that growing number of books that are quietly circulating among thoughtful people who are aware of the fragility of our civilization and the threat to all its values." John Fermatt cited Weaver's "courage and philosophical integrity" to challenge trends of scientism, the cult of progress, and the mass media. Reviewers especially liked Weaver's revolt against mass society. A consequence of World War II was that both the triumph of industrialism and the cradle-to-grave welfare state were complete. Weaver was not alone in noticing the enormous pressures placed on modern man in this new urban culture. Rises in mental illness, the breakup of family life, the phenomenon of a new, "alienated" man and the general unhappiness modern men experienced from giving more labor to the "global economy" and having less time for family life were baneful phenomena of the era, all captured brilliantly in this now-famous book.[19]

Other conservatives rallied to Weaver's defense. Willmoore Kendall nominated Weaver as "captain of the anti-liberal team" (a team that was indeed coming into its own). The book also caught the eye of a young Russell Kirk, who displayed it prominently in his East Lansing,

Michigan bookstore. Kirk invited Weaver to speak in East Lansing and the two began a friendship that lasted until Weaver's death. Although his fame and influence would eventually surpass Weaver's, Kirk immensely admired the author of *Ideas,* even considering him a lifelong mentor. Frank Meyer held similar sentiments. Decades later, Meyer praised the book as the *"fons et origin"* of modern conservativism. A former Communist party *appartchik* (at the same time Weaver was practicing socialism), Meyer called *Ideas Have Consequences* the most important single book in his own conversion from socialism to traditionalism. More importantly, the book also provided the inspiration for Meyer's own famous traditionalist/libertarian fusionist philosophy that Meyer hoped would unite these competing visions into a powerful political force.[20]

Meyer was correct about the impact of *Ideas Have Consequences.* The book did serve as a launching point for the post-World War II conservative movement. Conservatism—or at least opposition to the New Deal—did exist in the 1930s. But there were no journals such as *National Review* or *Modern Age* to serve as a platform for its thinkers. Seward Collins' *American Review* gave space for the Vanderbilt Agrarians to publish reviews and essays, but that brief partnership ended when Collins, in the mid-1930s, announced his sympathy for European fascism. Nor did conservatism gain much of a foothold in either political party. There were Republicans opposed to both the New Deal and potential American involvement in World War II. But the 1940 nomination of Wendell Wilkie (who gained further fame as the best-selling author of *One World*) would eventually highlight the political impotence of antiwar Republicans.

Still, that group of early conservatives was a hardy and courageous mixture of anti-New Deal small businessmen, anti-interventionist Midwesterners and Westerners, and Weaver's own Vanderbilt Agrarian mentors. Leading poets, critics, and novelists of the day—Robert Frost, T.S. Eliot, Edmund Wilson, Robinson Jeffers, William Saroyan, Kathleen Norris, Edgar Lee Masters, Maxwell Anderson, and Allen Tate to name serveral—opposed both the statism and foreign policy of the Roosevelt administration. But the successful prosecution of World War II smashed the "America First" movement and rendered American conservatism little more than an historical oddity. Or so it seemed.[21]

However, the final three chapters of *Ideas Have Consequences* did introduce the possibility of a fusion of existing conservative thought.

Weaver's support of private property as an bulwark against the whims of the political state formed the basis of his libertarianism. That he opposed state power is fairly evident in the pages of both *The Southern Tradition at Bay* and *Ideas Have Consequences*. Weaver was against the excesses of the state, but economic liberation did not mean an invitation to frivolity. He was also for maintaining ancient traditions and keeping natural distinctions of sex, age, class, and culture intact. One could hardly imagine Weaver defending totally free trade markets or open immigration borders. The strong case made for traditionalism in the chapters, "Piety and Justice" and "Distinction and Hierarchy" more than his libertarianism, was Weaver's greatest contribution to the conservative movement. His defense of agrarianism, his repeated assaults on all forms of mass culture and his call for a generational piety that would sustain ancient customs struck a powerful chord among traditionalists who shared Weaver's anxieties.

The conservativism of the 1930s and the post-World War II era wished to defend America's founding agrarian culture against, among other things, massive industrialism and the controls and regulations New Deal legislation placed on farmers and small businessmen. The destruction of thousands of acres of farm land in Tennessee and Alabama by the Tennessee Valley Authority is perhaps the most dramatic example of how juggernaut technology and state power revolutionized America. Before it became a Manhattan/Washington phenomenon, conservatism was truly a Middle America movement that championed small-town values against the workings of a centralized state. For instance, Jefferson the agrarian, rather than Jefferson the deist, would be the conservative model of great statesmanship.

All that the centralized state symbolized, including things that we take for granted such as public education, were seen by many conservatives as mortal threats to the country's distinctive small-town culture. If conservatism meant anything, it was as a movement to preserve Western civilization from a valueless, wholly material culture that threatened to overwhelm both Europe and North America. Thus, the educational curriculum must, above all, contain the study of Greek and Latin, the Bible, Shakespeare, Dante, St. Augustine: the literature that formed the basis of Western and as such, American civilization. Conservatives stood against any "new" ideas in education, especially the technical training and specialization that Weaver savaged in both *The Southern Tradition at Bay* and *Ideas Have Consequences*.

Russell Kirk has written that Weaver originally called the book, *The Fearful Descent*, preferring that title to "Ideas Have Consequences." Other scholars claim the book was in fact titled *The Adverse Descent*, a phrase not quite as urgent as the one Kirk gives. *The Fearful Descent* would have been a better title; it captures perfectly both the book's apocalyptic prose and prophetic warnings. Weaver intensely disliked "Ideas Have Consequences," so much so that he threatened to pull the book from publication. But cooler heads prevailed and Weaver accepted Couch's title. Considering how the phrase "ideas have consequences" has become a worn-out political cliche, one can sympathize with Weaver's original desire. Numerous politicians cite the phrase, mostly to mean that "ideas" (usually in the form of new government programs) always have (entirely good) consequences. "Ideas have consequences" is used to justify crime bills, education bills, "welfare reform," and numerous other federal spending programs. If "ideas have consequences" meant celebrating "democratic capitalism" or an "opportunity society" then Weaver would likely want no part of it. Chilton Williamson, Jr. once noted correctly that Weaver would reject a conservatism which applies endless government solutions to social ills.[22]

As it stood, *Ideas Have Consequences* launched Weaver's career. Now he was a nationally known intellectual who had suddenly attracted a legion of admirers. Weaver did not shy away from a public role; he lectured widely on behalf of the conservative cause, appearing on radio programs and as a regular contributor to *National Review* and *Modern Age*. Throughout the years, *Ideas Have Consequences* has stayed in print, but after the initial spate of publicity, it did not sell as well in succeeding decades. The people at the University of Chicago were not entirely happy with the book. In 1945, Chicago had also published Friedrich Hayek's famous tract against state planning, *The Road to Serfdom*. Now with *Ideas* causing a similar uproar, Chicago was getting a reputation for publishing reactionary texts. Obviously, the boys at Mr. Hutchins's university weren't happy with this development. When Mr. Couch left the press a few years later, Weaver lost his biggest supporter at Chicago. He would now have to look elsewhere to find publishers for other books.

While Chicago published a paperback edition of *Ideas* in 1959, the press never promoted the book with much vigor. They did not, for instance, champion *Ideas* as a publication that launched a major intellectual movement in America. *Ideas Have Consequences* is a less comprehensive book than Russell Kirk's *The Conservative Mind* (also a published dissertation), but like *Ideas*, it is acknowledged as one of the conservative movement's founding documents. *The Conservative Mind* has been promoted that way and continues to sell steadily year in and year out. With proper promotion, *Ideas* could have had the same long and fruitful life enjoyed by Kirk's magnum opus.

But for the time being, Weaver had to be delighted with the turn of events his career had taken. With one book, he established himself as a figure to be reckoned with; if Chicago didn't like having Weaver around, then other universities would be glad to have this important thinker on their faculty. However, in his next book, Weaver would change course slightly. He would continue his critique of modern culture, but this time by turning his attention to the power of the written and spoken word.

4

State Worship:
The Ethics of Rhetoric, Language Is Sermonic

Five years elapsed between the publication of *Ideas Have Conse-quences* and Weaver's next book, *The Ethics of Rhetoric*. *Ideas* brought Weaver some fame; as a result, speaking engagements and other ac-tivities gave him problems with finding time to write.[1] Still, Weaver continued to contribute reviews to *Commonweal, Sewanee Review, Georgia Review*, and other publications. He also wrote essays on rheto-ric for such scholarly journals as *College English* and the *Journal of General Education*.

More essays on rhetoric made up *The Ethics of Rhetoric*, a book that was an extension of "The Power of The Word" chapter in *Ideas Have Consequences*. In that chapter, Weaver attacked modern-day practitioners of semantics for injecting a destructive relativism into the study of rhetoric. Such litterateurs were the first deconstructionists, manipulating the language for their political purposes. Weaver also focused on the positive influence of rhetoric, citing Shelley's famous dictum that poets are "the unacknowledged legislators of the world." He called on educators to teach foreign translations to students, espe-cially to aspiring journalists. This practice would teach a greater ap-preciation of words and their true meanings.

Again, times have changed and none for the better. Translations are only sparingly taught at colleges and universities. Millions of young people each year receive college degrees without learning a foreign language, not to mention some mastery of Latin and Greek (once a prerequiste for all university students). Even in the 1940s and 1950s, poets like Eliot, Pound, Ransom, Frost, Robinson Jeffers, Wallace Stevens, and Theodore Roethke all enjoyed real fame in the world. Americans, in decent numbers, walked into bookstores to buy volumes of poetry by Frost or Jeffers. Some citizens did look to poets to offer eternal truths and wisdom on the human condition. There was some belief in the power of poetry, none of which exists today. All this makes Weaver's scholarship more valuable to us. If Richard Weaver had never written social criticism or studies of Southern culture, we would be poorer for it, but his essays on rhetoric alone gained him a devoted following as a courageous and important thinker.

Weaver knew that an age of specialization, which placed little emphasis on liberal arts education, was hostile to the study of rhetoric. Still, he plunged ahead writing, lecturing and teaching rhetoric, patiently arguing that it was "the most humanistic of the humanities," and recalling that as late as the nineteenth century, rhetoric was the most important discipline taught in the university. The teacher of rhetoric was expected to be a man of gifts and imagination, who could make words "even in prose take on wings."

In Weaver's time, citizens would stop to listen to a speech by Churchill or MacArthur; since then, the great rhetor has passed from the scene. *The Ethics of Rhetoric* and essays in *Language is Sermonic* amount in part to a rousing defense of rhetoric, not unlike the same rousing defense of private property in *Ideas Have Consequences.* Weaver never lost sight of rhetoric's hold on our lives. A true and noble rhetoric presents us with a proper view of man and a pleasing vision of culture. Just as important, the selfless rhetor moved men to action with his words, carrying with him the power to alter history.

Take the example of World War II. To Weaver, it was a battle wherein Germany first succumbed to the evil rhetoric of Hitler, with England being moved to action against him by the soaring words of Winston Churchill. Hitler had "persuaded the multitudes that his order was the 'new order,' i.e., the true potentiality." Hitler's images, according to Weaver, had no true dialectic. Yet "evil rhetoric is more of a force than no rhetoric at all." If Churchill had not supplied his own counter-rhetoric, then the "contest would have been lost by default." By offering visions of "green lit uplands of freedom," Churchill was able to move men to action. His vision was not one of abstractions—democracy, socialism, capitalism—but the metaphysical dream of a free British isle, one that also conjured up visions of blood and land. In short, England, once again, became a nation worth dying for. This alone was enough to wake the country out of its torpor and send its sons to the ramparts.[2]

Rhetoric was also an art form that flourished in the Old South. In *Ideas Have Consequences*, Weaver remarked that it was no accident that the nation's greatest creative political figures—Jefferson, Lincoln, Wilson—were all Southerners steeped in rhetoric and law and educated in the "Ciceronian tradition of eloquent wisdom." Fred Hobson wrote that Weaver "felt, he was a classical rhetor in part because he was first a Southerner. The two callings were related. His Southern legacy had taught him a reverence for the word, a respect for rhetoric which, in any case, was more 'Southern' than dialectic." As such, Weaver constantly used Southerners, including the Kentucky-born Lincoln, as examples of rhetors who argued as Churchill later did—from defintion and with vision.[3]

Before the forces of science and technology cheapened modes of communication, the rhetor, even if he was not an elected politician, was a cultural phenomenon, a natural leader of men. Henry Grady, for instance, was not an elected official, but his rhetoric alone moved the South to action once Reconstruction ended. In olden days, the rhetor was a "big man talking." The rhetor also spoke to audiences that shared a somber reading of history.

Indeed, a major theme in Weaver's study of rhetoric is the role of the audience. Time and time again, he points out that great orators can succeed only if they have great listeners. A giant may walk among us, but if the masses have been corrupted by selfish rhetors proclaiming that freedom and prosperity are birthrights, then they will also lack the imagination to understand selfless rhetoric. This theme is the continuation of Weaver's revolt against the masses. Decadent as we moderns have become, we can't even appreciate the old rhetoric. With his grand style and unspoiled audiences—the rhetor spoke with the "right of assumption"—the spaciousness of the old rhetoric was able to flourish.

The nineteenth-century orator spoke to an audience that understood certain historical truths. This is also why we have contempt for the old rhetoric. It offered no promises of economic security or social peace. Instead it dwelled on man's possibilities—and his limitations. A rhetoric grounded in history and large, colorful language puts our own cynical style to shame. The old rhetoric understood the pageantry and drama of man's existence. "The heroes in tragedies also talk bigger than life . . . this kind of speech comes to us as an admondition to us that there were giants in the earth before us, mighty men, men of renown." In early America, what did the orator and his audience understand?

> He was comfortably cirumstanced with reference to things he could "know" and presume everyone else to know in the same way. Freedom and morality were constants; the Constitution was the codification of all that was politically feasible; Christianity of all that was morally authorized. Rome stood as an exemplum of what may happen to nations; the American and French Revolutions had taught rules their necessary limitations. Civilization has thought over its thousands of years of history and has made some generalizations which are the premises of other arguments but which are not issues themselves. . . . Men were not condemned to repeat history, because they remembered its lessons.[4]

Rhetoric, at its best, also gives us a vision of culture. In *Visions of Order,* Weaver wrote that healthy cultures form a "tyrannizing image." In this instance, tyrannizing does not carry a negative connotation. It meant that a vibrant culture looks inward to the poetry, songs, religion and codes of conduct that shape it. John Bliese in his excellent study, "Rhetoric and The Tyrannizing Image" wrote that "[M]any of Weaver's rhetorical concepts are based on the notion of a tyrannizing image that provides a culture with its ideals and goals."[5]

In *Ethics,* Weaver cites Representative Charles Faulkner, an obscure nineteenth-century congressman from Virginia to give us a pleasing image of culture. The congressman praises the farmers of ancient Rome as men who were fit for the responsibilities of freedom. He celebrated the agrarian civilization that his own constituents were to inherit. Rep. Faulkner's description of the rural man is close to Weaver's description of the Vermont farmer in *Ideas Have Consequences:*

> If we look to the past or to the present we shall find that the permanent power of any nation has always been in proportion to its cultivation of the soil—those republics which during the earlier and middle ages, were indebted for their growth mainly to commerce, did for a moment . . . cast a dazzling splendor across the pathway of time; but they soon passed from among the powers of the earth, leaving behind them not a memorial of their proud and ephemeral destiny whilst other nations, which looked to the products of the soil for the elements of their strength, found in each successive year the unfailing sources of national aggrandizment and power. Of all the nations of antiquity, the Romans were most persistently devoted to agriculture, and many of the maxims taught by their experi-

ence and transmitted to use by their distinguished writers, are not unworthy . . . of the notice of the intelligent farmers of this valley. It was in their schools of country life—a *vita rustica*—as their own great orator informs us, that they imbibed those noble sentiments which rendered the Roman name more illustrious than all their famous victories, and there, that they acquired those habits of labor, frugality, justice and that high standard of moral virtue which made them the easy masters of their race.[6]

When leaders such as Faulkner spoke with a grand rhetoric that was grounded in history and invoked visions of liberty, the public responded. Interest in politics ran high in the early America. Average citizens felt politics did make a profound difference in their lives; they wanted to be active participants in what we blandly call the "democratic process." Common folk were not alienated from their leaders; a man could walk into the offices of his congressman at most times of the day and strike up a conversation.

Weaver praised the old oratory as a "polite style." The orator used logic, aesthetics, and epistemology to get his point across. With poetic images and historical references, he gave his audiences a true picture of man's dual nature. Freedom, for instance, was not a plea for "unity," (which means a large bureaucracy is right around the corner) but instead a condition that came with responsibilties. In short, his wide range made the early American orator a big man in the eyes of the common folk. The man who orated in the spaciousness Weaver celebrates gained stature as a man who could be entrusted with the leadership role. He was well-rounded in history, rhetoric and in the understanding of human nature—just as the education of the gentleman demanded.

A rhetor speaks from defintion or circumstances. He comes into the fray with set ideas, convictions, and a vision. Or else he argues merely from circumstances, looking at the situation and deciding whether his ideas are feasible or not. This led to Weaver's controversial comparison between Abraham Lincoln and Edmund Burke.

To Weaver, Lincoln is our model both as an ideal rhetor and political conservative. The Lincoln argument from definition was based on the idea of union and individual freedom. Using Lincoln as a model for conservatism may confuse the reader, perhaps not in the case of freedom, but certainly with the idea of a union. In *The Southern Tradition at Bay*, Lincoln is criticized as a "universalist" whose demand that the nation must be "all one thing or all the other" left no room for the particularisms of any culture. And as we have seen, the idea of a "union" as a fighting faith was once looked upon with great suspicion by citizens of the Old Republic. The same book also contained blistering criticism of Lincoln by Southern apologists, who attacked him as a tool of radical Republicans, as an opportunist who would adopt any position for political gain, as a revolutionary who idolized secular democracy and in general, as a vulgar backwoodsman who lacked the gentlemanly qualities of earlier American leaders.

The conservative intellectual movement that Weaver helped to found also formed their own suspicions about the Lincoln legacy. Frank Meyer, Willmoore Kendall, and especially M.E. Bradford were among the Weaver disciples who took Lincoln to task for waging total war that both destroyed the nation's founding anticentralizing doctrines and ushered in an age of state power that later manifested itself in the Right's own living enemy, the New Deal. This passage from Meyer's *The Conservative Mainstream* sums up the Old Right case against Lincoln:

> Were it not for the wounds that Lincoln inflicted upon the Constitution, it would have been infinitely more difficult for Franklin Roosevelt to carry through his revolution, for the coercive welfare state to come into being and bring about the conditions against which we are fighting today. Lincoln, I would maintain, undermined the constitutional safeguards of freedom as he opened the way to centralized government with all its attendant political evils.[7]

There is a different portrait of Lincoln as a magnanimous victor. Along with many historians, Weaver believed that if Lincoln had lived, reconstruction would have been avoided. The Reconstruction era of 1865–1877 has become the forgotten period in American history. Very few Americans know about carpetbag governors, scalawag legislators, military occupation, and long decades of Southern poverty. In "The South and the American Union," an increasingly bitter Weaver noted that while the U.S. embarked on an ambitious Marshall Plan for Japan and Germany following World War II, there was, in the 1870s, no such economic plan for the defeated South. However, by the late 1870s many Northerners had become disgusted by the treatment of the South by Radical Republicans. The North wanted to get on with the business of moneymaking and had no desire to keep their defeated brethren under military rule. The wholesale looting of Southern state treasuries was another scar on what Northerners believed was a righteous cause.

We have already discussed the famous deal of 1876 which ended reconstruction. The North, on social issues at least, allowed the South to handle its own unique problems. With the abolitionists no longer a political force, Northern politicians (most of whom, Lincoln included, had no use for the abolitionists in the first place) were more than willing to leave the South alone concerning racial matters. The focus on progress would now come through public education and economic prosperity. Still, it took most of the South a good fifty years to begin to catch up with the North economically.

More ominously, reconstruction proved how a mighty centralized state could—through undemocratic means—impose its will on any region of the country. Regional cultures—which Weaver always considered a bedrock of American civilization—now saw their cultural integrity threatened by the centralized state. The "debauchery, corruption, and political buffoonery" of the 1860s and 1870s set the stage for the "second reconstruction" of the 1950s and 1960s. Weaver firmly believed his fellow Kentuckian would never have brought down the hammer on the defeated South. There would be no occupying forces, no scalawag legislators, no interference in local elections. If Robert E. Lee gained even greater dignity in defeat, then the victorious Lincoln would have also soared to heights of legendary statesmanship.[8]

Why else is Lincoln, according to Weaver, the true American conservative? For one, he was unambiguous about individual freedom, while at the same time opposing the scorched-earth policies of the New England abolitionists. Lincoln's speeches insisted on complete fidelity to the Constitution (although this is also grounds of conservative criticism of him). He wanted individual freedom (at least as it was defined in nineteenth-century America), he articulated a vision of a free, prosperous union, but mainly, "the essence of Lincoln's doctrine was not the seeking of a middle, but reform according to law; that is, reform according to definition."

The defense of Lincoln did make Weaver an appealing figure to many Northern conservatives who otherwise might have been alienated by the Southern partisanship displayed in other Weaver books and essays. However, despite Weaver's best efforts, this essay doesn't make an overwhelming case for Lincoln the conservative. The charge that his war in the cause of an abstraction ("Union") sent America down the road towards empire abroad and a massive, centralized bureaucracy at home remains compelling. In addition, Weaver, writing in the 1950s, could not make the 1980s and 90s defense of Lincoln.

That is, his fervent support for private property made Lincoln a libertarian-leaning figure who understood the potential of a dynamic, growing economy. The case for arguing from definition—and from principle—is the only positive lesson we get from this essay.

Conservatives also experienced confusion over Weaver's critique of Edmund Burke. While split over the Lincoln legacy, the Old Right always viewed Burke as its favorite eighteenth-century philosopher. But for Weaver, Burke's sin was that he always argued from circumstances. He had no set convictions, only calculated responses to various political crises of the day. On the Irish question, on the future of the American colonies, on the British Empire's future in India, Burke never argued from principle. Instead, he asserted that the large Catholic population of Ireland, the bright commercial future of North America, and the rich cultural traditions of India all mandated that England give up its imperialistic designs on these territories.

Burke hated the metaphysical argument and therein lies another source of Weaver's criticism. Each man, according to Weaver, has his own metaphysical dream of the world. That dream is his idea of beauty—and how the world should be ordered and administered. It also determines what a man will live, fight, and die for. By discarding metaphysical argument, Burke, unlike Lincoln or Rep. Faulkner, could not articulate a vision of culture. Therefore, Burke—and his Whig party—never entered the political fray with a set of principles. They only argued from circumstances and since circumstances always change, the Whigs were doomed. They lacked the self-respect to hold onto even a small, but loyal constituency. As a current comparison the always explosive American political issue of abortion may be considered. Public opinion, in one era, generally runs against abortion—or at least abortion-on-demand. The anti-abortion issue is, for the most part, a political winner. A certain political party eagerly welcomes pro-life groups under its big tent. But a Supreme Court decision easing abortion restrictions galvanizes pro-abortion rights groups. Public opinion swings the other way and the same party which readily identified with anti-abortion constituencies now wants to drop the issue altogether, pleasing no one in the process. It was a similar lack of principle that also doomed the Whigs.

Weaver even thought that Burke's critique of the French Revolution—the latter's great claim to American conservative influence—was also seriously flawed. Burke, Weaver felt, only opposed the French

Revolution because he wanted to maintain the status quo. A defense of hierarchy, feudalism, agrarianism, and regional cultures against the destructive centralizing forces of "liberty, equality, and fraternity," was not part of Burke's program. Russell Kirk thought this was so much quibbling over Burke's important insights into the French Revolution. "If Mr. Weaver rejects Burke, then he must reject conservative principles generally," Kirk wrote, "But really there is no need to reject Burke on Mr. Weaver's own terms; for Burke though he sneered at 'abstractions,' praised genuine 'principle.'"[9]

Despite his low opinion of Burke's style, Weaver nevertheless cites his famous lament on that revolution's consequences.

> But the age of chivalry is gone. That of sophisters, economists, and calculators has succeeded, and the glory of Europe is extinguished forever. Never, never more shall we behold that generous loyalty to rank and sex, that proud submission, that dignified obedience, the subordination of the heart, which kept alive, even in servitude itself, the spirit of exalted freedom. The unbought grace of life, the cheap defense of nations, the nurse of manly sentiment, is gone! It is gone, that sensibility of principle, that chastity of honour, which felt a stain like a wound, which inspired courage whilst it mitigated ferocity, which ennobled whatever it touched, and under which vice itself lost half its evil, by losing all its grossness.[10]

An argument from circumstance? Weaver still thought so. Kirk, on the other hand, was the Right's preeminent Burke scholar. Indeed, he almost singlehandedly made the Irish legislator a guiding light for the post-World War II antimaterialistic Right. The reader is likely to agree with Weaver's friend from Michigan on the Burke question. The problem for Weaver is that Burke's eloquence is strong enough to disguise an alleged lack of principle. His rhetoric moves men to action, which, after all, is the most important goal of the rhetor.

The essay on Lincoln, likewise, won't change many minds. Those unreconstructed types who view Lincoln as an opportunist who delivered hammerblows against the Old Republic aren't likely to be moved by the argument from definition strategy. (Indeed, in the early 1960s, Willmoore Kendall and M.E. Bradford visited Weaver in Chicago. There they hoped to convince the philosopher to drop his pro-Lincoln stance.[11])

However, conservatives who revere Lincoln are given a new reason to honor the sixteenth president: in addition to claiming the moral high ground, Lincoln was a leader of unshakable principle and conviction. By championing Lincoln, Weaver is telling conservatives to argue from definition and not to fret so much about what public opinion polls have to say. More specifically, he is asking them to become a resolute opposition party to the reigning statism of the times.

The comparison between these two modes of argument does contain a powerful political lesson. By arguing from definition on subjects such as individual freedom and the idea of the union, Lincoln transformed the GOP into the dominant political party in America. Lincoln's style of argument was echoed by Theodore Roosevelt, insuring GOP success into the early decades of the twentieth century. But after the 1932 election, the GOP, cowed by the depression and President Roosevelt's charisma, sank back into the argument from circumstance. The GOP thus began its long era of minority party status while ceasing to offer much opposition to juggernaut socialism. From 1932 onward, the Democrats firmly identified themselves in Weaver's mind as the "socialist party," while the GOP, at best, was merely the "liberal party." Weaver's pithy definitions of both parties is a more sophisticated version of "there ain't a dime's worth of difference between them." "Me-too" Republicanism was thus born. The GOP hoped to win elections by promising economic prosperity and offering candidates that belonged to a "better class of people." They also focused on Democratic party shortcomings (whatever that might mean). But the GOP had no real alternative to the Democrats' enthusiastic embrace of an activist government.

Eventually, the party turned to the cult of personality. First, there was Alf Landon, the Middle American populist, followed by Wendell Willkie, Middle American internationalist. When this didn't work, the GOP tried Thomas Dewey, East Coast crimebuster. The party finally hit the jackpot with Dwight D. Eisenhower, the war hero who could have just as easily been nominated by the Democrats. But none of these gentlemen were opponents of the New Deal. At best, they could "manage" the welfare state better than free-spending Democrats.

The reader will notice how little has changed since Weaver first charged the GOP with political surrender forty years ago. (The welfare state will probably survive the current Republican party "revolutionaries." Yes, there was an earthquake in the 1994 elections. But from 1996–2002, the Democrats proposed $14 billion in federal spending, while the GOP budget will spend . . . $13 billion.) Weaver was not impressed with Eisenhower's politics. Writing in *National Review* after the 1956 elections, he scornfully noted that the "Eisenhower Party" (not the GOP) had emerged victorious, thus giving us four more years of "middle of the road" liberalism. The term "middle of the road" was a popular phrase in the 1950s. Perhaps it derived from Arthur Schlesinger's definition of liberalism as "the vital center." Liberalism was the only game in town, it could "adapt" to changing times, while conservatives were only right-wing reactionaries. Critics were right, at least, about the latter assertion. Conservatives like Weaver and Kirk wore the "reactionary" tag like a badge of honor.

Certainly Weaver would agree with those few present-day maverick pols who argue that the only things in the middle of the road are yellow strips and dead armadillos. Writing for *Human Events*, he noted that: "Middle-of-the-roadism is seldom anything more than short-sightedness. It is not an insight into political matters because it is wholly dependent upon what other parties say, or stand for. It takes its bearing from them. And far from being safe, it is just the spot to catch brickbats from both sides." In short, Weaver disliked the political culture of the 1950s. However, his sentiments were almost universally shared by a rejuvenated conservative movement that sprung up around *National Review*.[12]

Richard Weaver was a frustrated hill country Republican (much in the same way Donald Davidson and Robert Frost were frustrated conservative Democrats). But if there was one American politician from his era who Weaver admired, it was Ohio Senator Robert A. Taft. Even though he was a party leader and son of a former president, Taft, by the 1950s, had come to represent a dying breed in GOP politics. He was anti-New Deal, but he also opposed the formation of NATO and the entire welfare/warfare state that the Cold War ensured. With World War II over, some conservatives wanted to get on with the business of dismantling FDR's welfare state. Taft, while publicly disclaiming the conservative label, was the anti-New Deal Right's natural leader.

Taft was anticommunist, but he also saw the establishment of an American military empire overseas as the decisive triumph of New Deal socialism at home. He shared the belief of Weaver (and many other conservatives) that a nation powerful and expansionist abroad will use that same power in setting its domestic agenda. A military empire raises taxes, debases the currency, and cannot tolerate domestic political dissent. Individual liberties are severely threatened under such a regime. Thus a nation that establishes a global empire will also move to destroy those regional cultures which pose a threat to its hegemony. The old Soviet Union, for instance, sought to destroy regional cultures in its own vast state, outlawing religion and forcing massive Russian population transfers into numerous non-Russian "republics."

The senator made a strong bid for the 1952 GOP nomination, but his campaign was stopped cold by the East Coast establishment. Taft's defeat prompted his bitter and famous remark that since 1932 the entire GOP nominating process had been controlled entirely by the boys in the boardrooms at Chase Manhattan Bank. Wall Street had once again trumped Main Street. The American Empire had defeated a champion of the Old Republic and the nation remained safe for statism.

A political party that lacks principle will perish. A party that sticks to a principle, even if that means losing elections, will weather its defeats and quite possibly emerge victorious in a different era—and for the right reason to boot. As it happened, the 1980s saw conservatives who endorsed Weaver's call for an argument from definition. Barry Goldwater's 1964 landslide loss to Lyndon Johnson, they argued, really wasn't a defeat after all. True, they lost *that* campaign, but by wresting control of the party away from the East Coast establishment, the Republicans would finally define themselves as the party of anticommunism and limited government. This creed (along with the anti-tax sentiments of the late 1970s) carried the GOP to landslide victories in the 1980s. Republicans had lost a single election in 1964, but as conservatives remembered, they went down on principle. And so they rose to fight another day, eventually tasting the fruits of political victory.

Of course, the conservative triumphs of the 1980s themselves have been subject to strict historical revisionism. Some on the Right have looked at the continued high growth of government spending, the decline of middle class incomes and the revolution of multiculturalism; reluctantly declaring that the decade wasn't such a golden age after all. But Weaver's point remains; one hopes a rising generation will learn from past mistakes. The Republicans can argue from a principle that opposes statism or they can perish along with their Whig brethren.[13]

What Killed the Old Rhetoric?

Granted we are living in unheroic times. There are few orators capable of living up to the spaciousness of the old rhetoric; alienaton, despair, and a feeling of helplessness over the nation's mounting so-cial ills runs high. What killed the old rhetoric that Weaver so ad-mired? There was, for instance, the rhetoric of the social scientist who believed man could be perfected by both scientific means and govern-ment largess and thus left no room to examine man's complex nature. A creature who is a candidate for perfection is hardly a participant in the great drama between good and evil. We know man is naturally good and we—meaning the huge army of bureaucrats the social scien-tist worked in tandem with—will both perfect man and give him un-limited prosperity.

There is also the stereopticon; namely the modern journalism trans-mitted to us with the "shortest sentence of all." Journalism captured the imagination of the masses (through titillating and often dishonorable means), but it also destroyed the grandeur of the old rhetoric. Its sensationalism and short sentences did not allow for a visionary, imagi-native style. From journalism, the road leads downward to "sound bites," glib promises, and skeptical language by cynical leaders. And when politicians use short, cynical phrases ("Read my lips," "New kind of Democrat," "Morning in America,") designed only to temporarily win the affections of the public, then the masses, spoiled as they may be, understand all too well the skepticism coming from the top down.

It should not be overlooked that although the masses in any society are compartively ill-trained and ignorant, they are very quick to sense attitudes, through their native capacity as human beings. When attitudes change at the top of society, they are able to see that change long before they are able to describe it in any language of their own and in fact they can see it without ever doing that. The masses thus follow intellectual styles and more quickly than is often supposed, so that, in this particular case, when a general skepticism of predication sets in among the leaders of thought, the lower ranks are soon infected with the same thing.[14]

In our time, we can see how all this has come to full fruition. There has been resentment and violence—ethnic and racial tension, cities destroyed by riots and crime—all stemming in part from the demagogue's promise that the world owes us a living. But for the most part the American public has viewed the nation's condition with great cynicism. We have the lowest voter turnout among all Western and non-Western nations that hold occasional free elections. While our ancestors in all regions of the country would have met threats to liberty by taking their trusty muskets off the shelf, recent generations have reacted to the current crisis by becoming increasingly dispirited and surly. The shallow rhetoric of both parties—above all, a rhetoric that wishes to avoid explosive social and cultural issues (that is, it wishes to avoid controversy), has only succeeded in breaking the spirit of the people.

The Ethics of Rhetoric was published in 1953. As such, the book can be read as a scathing critique of 1950s culture. Ever since the 1970s, there has been great nostalgia in the United States for the 1950s. Some of it is understandable. There was low unemployment and little inflation. For young people, the middle-class dream—buying a home, living in a safe neighborhood, paying tuition for their children's education—was much more easily attainable than it is today. Americans, almost exclusively, bought automobiles made in Detroit. It was an age when a man could support a family on a single paycheck. The 1950s represented the last era of American dominance of the dreaded "global economy." The U.S. produced the lion's share of the world's GNP (up to 40 percent), while Europeans and Asians were still struggling to recover from the ruins of World War II.

The 1950s also saw rapid gains by forces of science and technology. Television quickly conquered the American living room. If radio and tabloid newspapers threatened to turn us into "mute recipients" to the propagandists of the Stereopticon, then one can only imagine what Weaver thought of the television age. Richard Weaver cared little for middle-class complacency. The exodus to suburbia hardly represented the strenuous or romantic ethos needed to overthrow the cradle-to-grave welfare state. Indeed, the ever-growing welfare/warfare state continued to dominate the nation's political culture. A young senator from Arizona named Barry Goldwater criticized the "dime store New Deal" politics of the Eisenhower administration, but otherwise, there was no great political opposition to modern liberalism. Once Robert Taft went down to defeat in 1952, Weaver's Republican party swung fully into line as tax collectors for the welfare state. Significantly, the gains made by technology and the centralized state were reflected in the modes of rhetoric.

If debased rhetoric does not drive us to cynicism and despair, then it becomes a mighty weapon, bludgeoning the masses into line. "Ultimate Terms of Contemporary Rhetoric" is Weaver's blistering critique of both modern rhetoric and the 1950s culture it created. It is a devastating essay; arguably the finest in the book, a brilliant illustration of how rhetoric intimidates and controls the masses. Consider some of the ultimate terms. There are the "god terms"—progress, science, fact, modern, efficient, American, un-American, history, allies. There are also the "devil terms"—prejudice, communism, fascism, Rebel, Tory. The "charismatic" terms are freedom, democracy, and U.S. The ultimate terms signify the triumph of totalitarianism in the twentieth century. To drive home the point, Weaver quotes George Orwell on political language:

> Even in the early decades of the twentieth century, telescoped words and phrases had been one of the characteristic features of political language; and it had been noticed that the tendency to use abbreviations of this kind was most marked in totalitarian countries and totalitarian organizations. Examples were such words as Nazi, Gestapo, Comintern, Inprecor, Agitprop.[15]

We have been cowed by the ultimate terms. The god terms made certain words unassailable. No one can question the goodness of democracy or progress. Nor can anyone politely ask what those terms mean—nor whether their current meaning is such a good thing. Who, for example, would even venture to define democracy? Does it mean every resident of the U.S. over a certain age being allowed to vote? The Founding Fathers; indeed, no eighteenth-or nineteenth-or many twentieth-century American political figures ever imagined a one-man, one-vote democracy. Does democracy mean bureaucrats and judges telling cities and states how their districts have to be drawn up? If the Founders opposed universal suffrage, does that make them unprogressive and therefore the bad guys that certain social malcontents claim they are?

Similarly, no one wants to be against progress. All politicians, for instance, strive to champion "progressive" policies. In our time, we have even seen the emergence of "progressive conservatives." But what does progress mean? If free-market economics brings prosperity, but erodes traditional societies, is that worth the price of progress? The quest for economic (i.e., technological) progress, while supporting "traditional values" hurled conservatism into a brier patch of contradictions that the movement has never resolved. Weaver, along with Kirk and others, would demand that the preservation of a traditional society take precedent over material prosperity. Other conservatives declared economic growth and free markets to be the movement's dominant guiding principles. When a term is unassailable, as Weaver also understood, it can take on any meaning its practitioners wish. Recall from *Ideas Have Consequences* that when modern man "saw institutions crumbling," he rationalized it with "talk of emancipation." Such things may happen all in the name of "progress."

This god term leads to other buzzwords—modern living, American (which is synonymous with modern living) and un-American. According to Weaver, "modern living" is a consequence of scientific progress; it entails all the luxuries of mid-twentieth-century American life. It signifies the life of ease and comfort our media masters have long promised us. Modern living is "efficient" living. This is a "no-nonsense" term pleasing to an era when "the nation's business is business." But Weaver steps back to remind us that in our own time murderous tyrants—Hitler, Mao, and Stalin—were also "efficient" in their own ways.

But modern living means American living. In the mid-twentieth century, no other standard of living seemed imaginable. The term "American" conjured up images of limitless freedom and prosperity. It meant that any nation or peoples which did not emulate post-World War II America were hopelessly backward and benighted. To become Americanized, then, must be the goal of all nations. This confirmed that a materialistically oriented American society is superior to all other cultures. Weaver knew that whenever a nation feels this way, trouble is down the road. Such a nation constantly seeks to impose its way of life on other countries. It has little patience with the particularisms of different cultures. Weaver opposed such cultural imperialism. If people in the Samoan Islands, for instance, prefer to keep their agrarian way of life, who are we in the "developed" world to tell them otherwise? Weaver's Confederate heritage firmly taught him to oppose imperialism, whether through military, economic, or cultural means.

Worst of all, worship of a vague "Americanism" causes us to sever the cultural ties between American and European civilization. The America that Weaver's ancestors helped to settle was an extension of Anglo-Saxon civilization. Those men sought to restore (by rebelling against King George) the liberties granted under Anglo-Saxon law. That was the entire meaning of our Revolutionary War—and also the foundation of American civilization. But now "America culture" was superior even to Anglo-Saxon culture. Weaver notes that when T.S. Eliot and Henry James rejected their American citizenship to become English subjects, Americans were incredulous. It was as if those men had committed "treason to history." The emergence of god terms represented a great swelling of postwar American pride and ego. Ever the somber philosopher, Weaver knew what followed the deadly sin of pride.

But it was "science" that Weaver saw as the most daunting of the god terms. To remind skeptics that "science says" or "science proves," Weaver noted, was the final word in any debate. Like modern education, democracy, and the contrasts between urban and rural life, the phenomenon of modern science was a theme that runs through all of Weaver's works. Though a false god, science's promise is irresistible. In effect, acolytes of science tell us: Look at your history. What good has come from the old ways? For centuries, mankind has suffered through wars, famine, poverty, destruction. Man has had to break his back to earn his daily bread. Science will come along to change all this. It will provide a prosperity so great as to alter human nature forever. With prosperity, comes "real peace." Man will no longer be the beast conceived in original sin. He will no longer make war on his brother. He will live in peace with his neighbor because science will satisfy his primordial longings. In short, science—even more so than democracy—will bring about the "end of history."

The famous 1927 Scopes "Monkey Trial" in Dayton, Tennessee, which Weaver dissected in "Dialectic and Rhetoric at Dayton, Tennessee" highlights the effectiveness of the god term science.

In the 1920s, the Tennessee state legislature passed a law mandating the teaching of creationism in that state's public schools. A young science teacher in Dayton, John Scopes, was put upon by outsiders to test the law by teaching Darwin's theory of evolution. After accepting the challenge and teaching some evolutionary theories, Mr. Scopes was duly arrested and put on trial. William Jennings Bryan, former secretary of state, a three-time presidential candidate, and the leading populist orator of his day, prosecuted the case for the state. The famous defense lawyer, Clarence Darrow, fresh from his victory in the notorious Leopold and Loeb murder trial, took Mr. Scopes' defense. The proponents of evolution were delighted. Now they would have a world stage to expose both the ignorance of the Tennessee law (and rural culture) and the rightness of their scientific revolution.

To be sure, the purpose of the essay is to show Bryan's correctness in arguing from a proper dialectic. The trial, Bryan patiently maintained, was about the ability of Tennessee to enforce its own law, not the merits of the law itself. (No one doubted its constitutionality.) Paeans to King Science were not relevant. Thus Bryan was the true champion of constitutional law and honest rhetoric.

Darrow, on the other hand, was exposed by Weaver as an ideologue who changed his dialectic to suit whatever case he was arguing. At the Leopold and Loeb trial, Darrow noted that the defendants were inspired to murder young Bobby Franks after reading Friedrich Nietzsche in books borrowed from a public library. That being so, weren't the taxpayers of Chicago partially guilty for allowing such dangerous books in their library? With the Scopes trial, Darrow's argument changed. Evolution was the "truth" and the Tennessee legislature had no "right" to suppress the truth. In Chicago, however, public suppression of Nietzsche might have saved a human life.[16]

Still, the trial assured science's place as the king of all god terms. Darrow called up expert after expert, each of whom sang the praises of science and Darwinism. The future is with science, they argued. Science is the key to knowledge and prosperity. The teaching of evolution was necessary to the understanding of science. Without evolution, young people in Tennessee were being deprived of scientific knowledge; in short, revelations that would assure them a bright future. According to Weaver, the trial was no longer about the legitimacy of laws passed by a sovereign state legislature, but aimed instead to expose the backwardness of creationism. Tennessee was ridiculed by the entire Western world as a yahoo state; one that stood in the way of a glorious future made possible by the wonders of science. The god term progress also made its way into the debate. Science equals progress and progress means material prosperity. So we must have science, and not religion, in the classroom.

The argument worked brilliantly. For the record, Scopes was found guilty of violating state law and fined $100. More importantly, the superiority of science and progress were brought to the stubborn backwoods of America. The "New South" elite in politics, academia, and journalism all speeded up their efforts to lead the region towards industrialism and away from its agararian past. The president of Vanderbilt University, for instance, remarked that under his tenure, he wanted to graduate bankers and not farmers. There was some irony in all this. The Vanderbilt administration, through no encouragement of its own, had also seen an important modernist poetry movement spring up on its grounds. The Dayton trial inspired those "Fugitive" poets and novelists—John Crowe Ransom, Allen Tate, Donald Davidson, Robert Penn Warren, and Andrew Lytle—to come together now as proponents of agrarianism. That effort resulted in *I'll Take My Stand,* a defense of regional cultures so compelling that it attracted several generations of disciples, including the young Richard Weaver.

Just as no one can gainsay god terms, who wants to be tagged with a devil term? Such terms are rhetoric's big scarlet letter. When a man is denounced with a devil term, he is, for all purposes, being read out of polite society. In *Ideas Have Consequences,* Weaver spoke of men well versed in the art of rhetoric as being "admired or feared." A powerful rhetor can be admired if he speaks to a great audience, such as when early American rhetors spoke to audiences that understood lessons of history, responsibilities of freedom, and the sanctity of the U.S. Constitution. However, the powerful rhetor is feared by a regime that wants to consolidate power. Devil terms must then be applied to shoot down this "dangerous" individual. Devil terms, Weaver makes clear, are used to cut off debate and discussion. If a man, for instance, is "prejudiced" (never mind what he is "prejudiced" against), then he is a danger to society and must be treated that way. The *ad hoc* uses of these terms is meant to intimidate both the target and the public. In recent decades, devil terms have been used with stunning regularity against maverick politicans who threaten the status quo. If such devil terms as "isolationist," "protectionist," "nativist," don't create the desired result, then the ultimate terms of our times, "racist," fascist," "neo-Nazi" are in order. In all instances, however, the use of ultimate terms assumes there is a docile public willing to roll over and do as they are told.

Some charasmatic terms are "U.S." and "freedom." There are similiarites between them and god terms like "American." A man of the Old Republic, Weaver was both baffled and angry at the disasterous turns postwar America had taken. Words like freedom and U.S. do carry important connotations. But as with democracy, we must ask what they mean to modern-day citizens. Weaver is here to tell us that what we call "freedom" isn't necessarily the real article. Freedom, for eighteenth-and nineteenth-century Americans who settled the frontiers in the South, Midwest, and Far West, meant something far different from the same term we moderns pledge allegiance to. Still, as Weaver noted: "The fact that what the American pioneer considered freedom has become wholly impossible to the modern apartment-dwelling metropolitan seems not to have damaged its potency."[17]

One can go further. Freedom to earlier generations meant owning property; it signified a time when a man built his house (and paid no mortgage), plowed his land, chopped his own firewood, and more often than not, didn't send his children to public schools. In many cases, there were no public schools—people didn't want them. Churches usually provided what education Americans wanted for their children. Freedom, Weaver reminded his readers, did not mean a two-bedroom apartment in a large city (or perhaps a ranch-style house in the sub-urbs). It did mean men and women settling the frontier, battling hostile elements, and building a life free from state interference. Such a life also defined the god term democracy.

Indeed, the term "democratic living"—minding one's business, being part of a community, and living up to the responsibilities of free-dom—was a popular phrase from the Old Republic; one that has also disappeared in our time. Because it meant freedom from dependency, "democratic living" was often used to define American liberty. The Vermont farmer from *Ideas Have Consequences* who could say No to the Leviathan state was a free man. The man in megalopolis at the mercy of local demagogues is not. As such, the definition of what it means to be an American has changed dramatically. Weaver notices that when we define "American," terms of "ruggedness and self-suffiency" are no longer used. For instance, "In the space of fifty years or less we have seen the phrase "two-fisted American" pass from the category of highly effective images to that of comic anachronisms."[18]

Instead, as Weaver ruefully makes clear, a whole new America has been created by a bureaucracy with a dialectic all its own. The abbre-viations of the bureaucracy—including U.S., but also well-known terms such as FBI, WPA, OSS, FDIC, RTC—all "confer charismatic author-ity." Abbreviated terms have their purposes. We are intimidated by the state. But we also stand in awe of its power and promise. We can't live without the government we profess to despise. Such terms signify a benevolent state that is all-powerful, but also all-caring and here to deliver us from want. They also are meant to steer a cynical and docile public towards state worship. Here is the book's finest example of how abbreviations are powerful enough to change the character of entire nation:

I seldom read the abbreviation "US" in the newspapers without wincing at the complete arrogance of its rhetorical tone. Daily we see "US Cracks Down on

Communists"; "US Gives OK to Atomic Weapons"; "US Shocked by Death of Official." Who or what is this "US"? It is clear that "US" does not suggest a union of forty eight states having republican forms of government and held together by a constitution of expressly delimited authority. It suggests rather an abstract force out of a new world of forces, whose will is law and whom the individual citizen has no way to placate. Consider the individual citizen confronted by "US" or "FBI." As long as terms stand for identifiable organs of government, the citizen feels that he knows the world he moves around in. But when the forces of government are referred to by these bloodless abstractions, he cannot avoid feeling that they are one thing and he another.[19]

Like the conservatism he helped to found, Weaver's cause was to dismantle a destructuve Leviathan state and replace it with all the proper functions of the Old Republic. A constitution that protected the integrity of regional cultures and acknowledged man's evil instincts, the aristocracy of achievement, and a nation made by frontiersmen and yeoman farmers—that was Richard Weaver's America. By assailing the charasmatic term "US," the man from Weaverville is describing a nation he could no longer recognize—and also one he held little hope for.

Rhetoric, even in its basest form, matters. The twentieth-century Left vigorously supported a large and activist state and conservatives put up no real political opposition. Weaver despised the conformity of the 1950s and looked elsewhere for the American ideal. When he compares the "ruggedness and self-sufficiency" of the American pioneer to the apartment dweller in megalopolis, Weaver is saying that we have not only lost our freedom, worse yet, we don't even know what the term once signified. Americans were hardly living strenuously or romantically in the 1950s. To make matters worse, the ultimate terms worked to smear dissent, create false gods, cut off serious debate on important philosophical issues and basically assure us that Big Brother is working diligently for our own good. Such a rhetorical campaign has achieved an all-too-easy success.

The Ethics of Rhetoric was less well received than *Ideas Have Consequences*. Still, it consolidated Weaver's position as one of the leading lights of the intellectual Right. Reviewing the book along with Robert Nisbet's *The Quest for Community,* Russell Kirk praised Weaver as "one of the most courageous men in America." According to Kirk, the value of *The Ethics of Rhetoric* was its unswerving devotion to truthful rhetoric, as opposed to language as a "mere device for expression of sensations." Kirk added that distinguishing "god" terms from the true meaning of words and also "distinguishing Economic Man from the civil social person," would, if successful, hold enormous benefits; mainly, in creating civil societies that "prefer Justice over a dubious 'Efficiency.'"[20]

Thomas Landess was even more effusive. Many years later, he wrote that the book has the power to "alter the thinking of an entire generation"; its value being that "rhetoric and thought go hand in hand and that together they constitute the most vital informing force in the political order."[21]

Both Kirk and Landess allude to Weaver's search for truth in the ultimate terms that define our culture. A serious debate on the meaning of democracy, freedom and the uses of a bureaucracy might lead the country back to its founding principles. But as Weaver noted many times, a great orator needs a great audience. If truth in the ultimate terms were ever debated, it would first have to be received by a virtuous people.

5

The Conservative's Sage:
Life Without Prejudice and Other Essays

By the mid-1950s, Richard Weaver had settled into a familiar working routine and had established himself as a respected member of the
University of Chicago's English Department. In 1949, for instance, he
was awarded the Quantrell Prize as the university's outstanding teacher
for that year. He also continued to prove himself as a writer with an
impressive breadth of interest and skills. Essays on Southern culture
appeared in various scholarly journals. In addition, Weaver continued
to write and lecture on rhetoric and education. *The Ethics Of Rhetoric*
was followed by the 1957 publication *Composition*, a textbook which
was revised in 1967.

There was also Weaver the conservative sage. The late 1940s and
1950s were a time of rapid conservative intellectual ferment in America.
Along with *Ideas Have Consequences,* Hayek's *The Road To Serfdom,*
Kirk's *The Conservative Mind,* Whittaker Chambers's *Witness,* and
William F. Buckley's *God and Man at Yale* were other publishing
events that brought this loosely-defined group of traditionalists and
libertarians together. In the 1950s, as Buckley remembered it, there
were eight weeklies of opinion circulating in the country, all of them
liberal. But with the inauguration of Buckley's own *National Review*
in 1955 and Kirk's *Modern Age* in 1957, conservatives now had both a
weekly and an intellectual quarterly to rally around (*National Review*
eventually became a biweekly). Both Buckley and Kirk solicited work
from a distinguished roster of writers whose work had tagged them as

reactionary. John Chamberlain, John Dos Passos, Frank Meyer, James Burnham, Willmoore Kendall, and Chambers all became regular contributors to *National Review*. Weaver himself contributed to both publications. His "Life Without Prejudice" was the first essay to appear in the inaugural number of *Modern Age*.

The highlight of Weaver's years in the conservative movement came in 1962 when he was given a special award from The Young Americans For Freedom at a huge rally in New York's old Madison Square Garden. There the unassuming professor shared the same stage with such famous political figures as former president Herbert Hoover, South Carolina Senator Strom Thurmond, and the soon-to-be Republican nominee for president, Senator Barry Goldwater. With several family members from Weaverville and elsewhere present, Weaver gave a short, but urgent speech on the meaning of liberty and its precarious existence in the modern world, and the debasement of man in a world made safe for statism:

> It is our traditional belief that man was given liberty to ennoble him. We may infer that those who would take his liberty away have the opposite purpose of degrading him. Too much is being said today about the dignity of man without realization that the dignity of man means the *worth* of man. There can be no worth of man unless there is an inviolable area of freedom in which he can assure the stature of a man and exercise choice in regard to his work, his associates, his use of his earnings, his way of life. Little by little this area has been traded away in return for plausible gifts and subventions, urged on by slogans. Now we are at a point where regimentation, which used to be suggested with apologies, comes couched in the language of prerogative. The past shows unvaryingly that when a people's freedom disappears, it goes not with a bang, but in silence amid the comfort of being cared for. That is the dire peril in the present trend toward statism. If freedom is not found accompanied by a willingness to resist, and to reject favors, rather than to give up what is intangible but precarious, it will not long be found at all.[1]

So unlike Hayek who would later write a famous essay explaining "Why I am Not a Conservative," Weaver embraced what Clinton Rossitor dubbed "the thankless persuasion." Weaver's work represented a conservatism that opposed the entire thrust of twentieth-century liberalism. This entailed not only opposition to economic revolution (Social Security, public works programs, business regulations, and the entire welfare state apparatus); conservatives of Weaver's era also confronted more controversial policies. They were anticommunist, but against the idea of an American empire; many opposed the formation of the NATO alliance and nearly all vehemently disliked

American participation in the United Nations. Remnants of the 1930s-style isolationism were still strong in the 1950s.

Conservatives of Weaver's era also had to contend with the revolutionary jurisprudence of the Warren Court. Still holding the banner of the Tenth Amendment, they opposed attempts by the federal government and the Supreme Court to interfere in the South's public school system. Weaver never formally declared his opposition to the *Brown vs. Board of Education* ruling on public school desegregation, but in "The South and the American Union" he expressed the prevailing conservative sentiment when he wrote: "The South knows that in wide areas a forced integration would produce tensions fatal to the success of education....The South's decision to resist the new forward motion of the centralizing and regimenting impulse has won it support in the North among those who see the issue of authority as transcending this particular application."[2]

In short, Northerners had sympathy for a movement that resisted social engineering schemes, which in time, might come to dominate the political culture in their region as well. For Weaver and other conservatives, the explosive debate wasn't just about desegregation but the whole idea of the federal government (and un-elected judges) extending its tentacles into "the sovereign states," in effect setting policy on delicate social issues for the rest of the country. Or as Weaver would later write: "The same charges of inequity leveled against the Southern regime will be leveled against capitalism, private property, the family and even individuality."

But more than legal issues were at stake as well. In *Visions of Order*, Weaver went further, angrily claiming that "the attempt to 'integrate' culturally distinct elements by court action...originate[s] in ignorance, if not in a suicidal determination to write an end to the heritage of Western culture." This is bold language, but typical of Weaver's talent for jumping into controversies later generations of conservatives would happily ignore. Weaver accurately predicted that the second reconstruction was about more than federal civil rights or voting rights legislation. It soon represented a full-scale assault on the nation's founding Western heritage, an ideology most starkly exemplified by today's aggressive acolytes of multiculturalism and political correctness.

The Old Right counterattack on the Warren Court revolution eventually fell out of favor with reigning conservative dogma. The

Eisenhower-Kennedy-Johnson era Right fought battles that conservatives of the eighties and nineties would repudiate and deem dishonorable. Some form of Federal state power was needed, they readily agreed, to deal with more "backward" elements of American society. By the early 1980s, conservatism had become almost strictly a political movement, concerned with their alleged clout inside the Republican party. Weaver was a Republican, but his contribution was more philosophical and in the context of the 1950s, more reactionary—a description that could be applied to nearly all the early contributors to *National Review* and *Modern Age*.

For Weaver, conservatism was acceptable as a hardheaded faith that accepted distinctions and a hierarchy. Conservatives and libertarians believe "that there is an order of things which will largely take care of itself if you leave it alone." Conservatives understood man's evil instincts. In politics, they accepted John C. Calhoun's interpretation of the U.S. Constitution as a "negative document," a series of "thou shall nots, specifically in the ways in which the liberties of individuals and of groups are not to be invaded." The conservative tolerates "diversity of his life and opinion" and sees such diversity as healthy to a free society. But conservatives were mainly traditionalists; they largely accepted the world handed down to them by their forefathers:

> It is my contention that a conservative is a realist, who believes that there is a structure of reality independent of his own will and desire. He believes that there is a creation which was here before him, which exists now not by just his sufferance, and which will be here after he's gone. This structure consists not merely of the great physical world but also of many laws, principles, and regulations which control human behavior. Though this reality is independent of the individual, it is not hostile to him. It is in fact amenable by him in many ways. But it cannot be changed radically and arbitrarily. This is the cardinal point. The conservative holds that man in this world cannot make his will his law without any regard to limits and to the fixed nature of things.[3]

Weaver's politics were primarily cultural. No discussion here of economics or foreign policy, although anticommunism soon became the single defining characteristic of American conservativism. When the subject was culture, however, ruminations on the decline of American education were, at least for most conservatives, never far behind. As we have noticed, public education in America was strictly a twentieth-century phenomenon. Prior to this century, primary and secondary public schools had little support in both the United States and through-

out the Western world. Early America was an age when home-schooling, at least as we understand it, reigned supreme. In Weaver's view,
"mass education" was one of the baneful consequences of an urban,
industrial society.

Each Weaver volume says something about education (and other
modern-day phenomena such as democracy, total war, the idea of
equality). With each work, the criticism reached newer and more mature heights. Weaver's 1957 essay, "Education and the Individual" is
the author's definitive statement on a subject he spent a lifetime pursuing. A teacher on the university level for over twenty years, and a
beneficiary (through his own determination) of a first-class liberal arts
education, Weaver, like Ransom, Kirk, and many other traditionalists,
was alarmed at the rapid decline of liberal education in America. In
"Education and the Individual," Weaver comes to terms with the idea
of mass education. This may be a weakness; in the long run, traditionalists will probably give up on public education altogether. But in
Weaver's day, there was still plenty of optimism (at least among taxpayers) that public schools could work.

The essay, like much of Weaver's work, is both a rousing defense
of individualism and an unrelenting attack on the conformity of the
post-World War II era. The philosopher crosses swords with John
Dewey, the famed liberal educator and longtime *bete noire* of the
American Right. The individualist approach recommended here is similar to a European-style education: at a certain age, each student either
learns a trade or goes on to a higher liberal arts education. Each
student should become a master in their own field, with a feeling (as
opposed to a meaningless "self-esteem") of real accomplishment.

To Weaver this was an "aristocratic" approach. "Inner personality,"
likewise, was an important achievement. From personality comes individualism. From individualism comes the discriminating citizen capable of becoming a free man in a free society. The discriminating
individual, at least, could hardly become a flunky for the demagogue
in megalopolis. Dewey, on the other hand, saw "inner personality" as
a sign of "social division." Inner personality forms the free-thinking
individual who may reject the state-controlled utopia Dewey and his
followers envisioned. Right from the beginning, Weaver understood
that modern-day public education was in part an ambitious attempt to
create generations of little social democrats.

Like all great Weaver essays, "Education and The Individual" remains memorable for its withering assaults on conventional wisdom. Both the attack on "progress" and the spoiled masses are outgrowths of themes first broached in *Ideas Have Consequences*. Progressives (radicals or liberals as Weaver also called them) come in for the lion's share of blame. More than anything, modern educators showed unremitting hatred for the past: the result has been several generations of sheer zombies; students with no knowledge of history, literature, or philosophy. Instead, young people were indoctrinated to toe the liberal line.

As with modern-day advertisers, progressive educators denied that real life involves "anxiety, strenuous self-sacrifice, [and man's] friction with his environment." Instead, they opted for "self-esteem" and "self-adjustment." However, great people throughout the ages—Socrates and Jesus Christ to name two Weaver examples—were quite maladjusted to their environment and their times. They also were in great friction and conflict with the ruling elites of those days. Today's vision of "happiness" was to Weaver just a sappy journalistic word, a "flabby" term that only meant a mindless conformity. Creative people are not always happy, he reminds us, but their happiness is of a very intense kind achieved through strenuous activity. Creativity is impossible in a feel-good environment where only "self-esteem" is important. Such criticisms have been repeated by other conservatives on countless occasions over the past seven decades.

Progressives, Weaver claimed, also use history as a social science, "turning their backs upon those subjects which throughout civilized history have provided the foundation of culture and of intellectual distinction." They disdain real intellectual discourse, preferring instead to teach "frivolous subjects such as dating patterns of teenagers" (that was thirty-five years ago; today's readers can substitute even more preposterous examples) rather than "the rise and fall of nations or the nature of man." Worst of all, progressives want state control over education; seeking to lord it over the entire nation's educational affairs, they would (and did) create a "Federal Education System" in Washington, D.C.

Such progressives were in many respects, the forerunners of today's multiculturalists. They did not specifically attack the Western tradition as a racist, sexist, oppressive civilization. Instead they saw history, including Western history, as bunk, something made irrelevant by the glories of social democracy. Since the state can save us, we can continue to dismiss the past as one large error and banish its hard lessons of tragedy and man's limitations from the classroom.

But the American public is also taken to task by Weaver for expecting too much from their schools. The industrialized age brought popular support for public schools. That may be tolerable, but Americans had grown soft in their expectations for public and private education. Education, Weaver noticed, was now either viewed as a springboard into the middle class or as a magic cure-all for society's ills. Crime, poverty, an "unskilled" labor force—all can be cured by improving public schools. In short, a wholly materialist view of education has triumphed.

It has been decades, many decades since the purpose of education was to produce Christian gentlemen. A cynic may look at the dismal standards of American education and declare that it has also been many decades since parents sent their children to college to receive the old "education of the gentleman." Who sends their children to college today to read Plato, Aristotle, Shakespeare, the Bible? Such an education is not deemed practical for a future made by science and technology. This dismal development also explains why the multiculturalists have had such an easy time of it. In the past, the "Western Civ" curriculum was banished for practical reasons (what kind of job can you get by reading Dante, Virgil, etc.?); it can also be banished now for ideological reasons (dead white males representing a great evil in the world). Weaver did not live to see this evil full flowering of progressive thought, but he accurately and relentlessly prophesied where an egalitarian view of education would lead us.

The state of American education has long bedeviled and frustrated the post-War Right. The rise of political correctness on the American campus has produced so many zany excesses ("woman" spelled "womyn," universities insisting on same-sex lavatories, etc.) that the conservative counter-attack became too easy and as such, too lazy. Broadsides against political correctness have turned into a cottage industry of its own.

Conservatives, as always, have been divided on America's crisis in education. In the 1950s, Weaver, Davidson and the editors of *National Review* opposed the *Brown vs. Board of Education* ruling on both cultural and constitutional grounds. Weaver warned against a "Federal Department of Education" that would wrestle local control of schools away from states and communities and as such, destroy the particularisms of the country's richly diverse regional cultures. Indeed in 1980, presidential candidate Ronald Reagan promised to abolish the newly created Department of Education. After those battles were (barely) fought and lost, the Right tried different tactics: supporting "school choice," vouchers enabling poor children to attend wealthy private schools, and tuition tax cut credits for parents who send their children to religious schools. By the 1990s, home-schooling had crept back onto the agenda, completing a circle of sorts.

As far as the battle of the books is concerned, it suffices to say that this controversy wasn't nearly as heated in Weaver's time as it is today. Still, Weaver laid down his own core curriculum. The emphasis was on math, philosophy, language, and history. All four subjects stress discipline and self-mastery. From mathematics, symbols which form the "basis of our thinking" are taught. A study of language teaches young people how to think; it is the "superior organization of man's self-ordering growth."

But the most passionate plea came for a proper study of history. Here the grand pageantry of human drama unfolds. Rather than a suffocating "social science," history (like literature) shows man in all his glory and folly. It is the "record of the race," which teaches man "not to be self-indulgent." Weaver liked to cite Byron: History in all its glory, contains but one page. In short, the struggle for man's soul, the rise and fall of nations—that, not "self-adjustment," is history. We are not a race of "new men," but individuals condemned to live in history, with all the struggles and tribulations that involves. Santayana's famous statement, "those who forget history are condemned to repeat it" has long been turned into a dreadful cliche, but Weaver would embrace it wholeheartedly. Cliches do carry great truths; that's how they earn the term in the first place.

Above all, Weaver kept his focus on the individual. He ends the essay with a stern rejoinder from Socrates that "the unexamined life is not worth living." Weaver's own life was such an example. He studied widely—the University of Kentucky, Vanderbilt, Louisiana State University; with seminars at the University of Virginia, Harvard, and the Sorbonne in Paris. Admittedly, this was an education few of us could afford. But Weaver was also a self-taught man. As a youth, he worked his way through prep school; while attending Vanderbilt, he paid the bills with a teaching fellowship.

In *The Southern Tradition at Bay*, Weaver reminds us that history is part of the liberal arts; all sides of a story need to be examined—we can't always rely on the winning side's account. By attacking modernism in an age where the centralized state stood all-powerful and generally unopposed, Weaver inspired the creation of an intellectual movement against the reigning statism of the day. That took great audacity—and no little amount of courage, too. On the subject of education, Weaver is asking the patient to heal thyself; something that can only come through living the strenuous life.

Defining Culture

Another important statement collected in *Life Without Prejudice* was Weaver's remarkable *tour de force* on the meaning of culture itself, a 1961 essay entitled "The Importance of Cultural Freedom." Here, all that Weaver learned about culture from his study of ancient Athens and Rome, the Middle Ages and the Old South comes together in the author's own definitive statement on the subject.

Since Weaver himself was the "doctor of culture" he referred to in *Visions of Order*, this essay is one of the more important and more lasting of his short, but prolific career. And since conservatives are at least nominally fighting the cultural wars, this essay lays out the enormous stakes for them. It also puts Washington-Manhattan conservatives in their place, explaining in so many words that American culture cannot be micromanaged from Washington, D.C. The essay's beginning sets the tone, containing a particularly eloquent definition of culture. In one paragraph, Weaver is able to say why "it's the culture, stupid" is more important than anything else to the survival of a nation.

Culture in its formal definition is one of the fulfillments of the psychic needs of man. The human being is a focal point of consciousness who looks with wondering eyes upon the universe into which he is born a kind of stranger. No other being, as far as we can tell, feels the same amount of tension between himself and the surroundings in which he must pass his existence. His kind of awareness is accompanied by degrees of restlessness and pain and it is absolutely necessary, as we must infer from the historical record, that he do something to humanize his vision and to cognize in special ways his relation to these surroundings. This he does by creating what is called a culture.[4]

A thousand years from now, a man could read that passage to an audience and be greeted with unanimous approval.

How do cultures come about? Weaver maintains they can only exist within the consensus of a civilized community. Cultures are identified by many factors, including religion, race, climate, geography, language, poetry, songs and mythology. From a well-defined culture springs forth the customs, codes of conduct and laws those members agree to live under.

Specifically, all healthy cultures are regional and we can infer, either agrarian or small town. For instance, the cultures of New Hampshire, East Tennessee, Montana, West Texas, and Northern Michigan are all something regional and traditional. They are cultures built and nurtured over a long period of time (not decades, but at least two centuries) giving them distinct identities. Laws on our own endlessly explosive social issues (school prayer, abortion, death penalty, even income taxes) usually reflect religious traditions. Weaver reminds us that culture, not economics, drives the politics of those distinct regions, all of which share the same desire to be left alone by the centralized state.[5]

Who opposes regional cultures? Our enemy, as Albert Jay Nock pointed out years ago, remains the state. But when Weaver takes up his sword against "big government," it is the far-off, always meddlesome centralized apparatus he is attacking. Weaver did not wish to abolish the state. While it must be confronted when it steps out of its constitutional bounds, the state has its purpose. Weaver's libertarianism had its limits: we need the state to regulate excessive behavior. Typically, Weaver uses a controversial example, in this case, the role of censorship and the state. Extreme conditions would have to materialize for Weaver to endorse censorship, but he does not completely rule it out. Censorship may occur when the ruling state is insecure and must bar great literature like *Huckleberry Finn*. Weaver would not endorse such actions, but he could envision censorship as less an attack on artistic integrity, than a form of self-defense.[6]

For instance, he bluntly states that a "completely open society" is untenable (if not suicidal). What does this mean? A completely open society can mean that alien ideas and doctrines will eventually crash the barriers of an agreed-upon culture. In short, censorship is only necessary when a society is "out of joint itself." The spread of obscenity, in its various forms, makes some form of censorship desirable. Obscenity only comes into being when a society has become spoiled, decadent, and inhumane. Weaver admits he had not been able yet to deal with "the problem of how the state should protect minors from things they are not yet ready to cope with." But this essay was written in 1961 and Weaver could not foresee the spread of obscenity from Times Square and the streets of Chicago to the local movie houses and prime-time television. Had he lived to see the invasion of the red-light districts into the American living room, Weaver might have declared American culture itself to be "out of joint" and a candidate for some forms of censorship.

The censorship debate only illustrates one problem that a "completely open society" brings about. In the Cold War years, the idea of an open society held great attraction to Western intellectuals; it was a pleasing alternative to the brutal totalitarian states in the Soviet Empire. From an "open society" it is a very short step to open markets (free trade) and open immigration borders. For instance, the Committee for the Free World, an anticommunist organization that flourished during the 1980s, used liberal immigration policies as a way to measure the progress of the world's free nations.

An "open society," by these lights, has proved very troublesome to traditionalists. What do doctrines of free markets and open borders mean to traditional societies, not to mention economic and social stability? Weaver did not live to see how massive immigration from non-Western cultures into the United States and Europe helped to spark political unrest in democracies across the Western world. On this single issue, which has been an occasion for bitter conservative warfare, we can refer to Weaver's study of Henry Grady who in the late nineteenth century, urged Southerners not to accept immigrants that might "bring in heresies and discordant ideas." There are negative aspects to the ideology of an open society, and this too is a cause for great contention among modern conservatism's various factions.

Weaver's libertarian instincts shine through in this essay, but it was only one aspect, and not the dominant one, of his philosophy. Like Russell Kirk, Weaver would have little use for current-day libertarians. This breed opposes the state for economic reasons alone—lower taxes, less regulation, less government means a booming economy; a booming economy means individual and political freedom. The preservation of traditional societies (if they even believe there is such a thing as a traditional society) usually doesn't enter the equation. Rather the emphasis is on "individual freedom." For Weaver, conservatism meant much more than that.

Still, Weaver and libertarians could break bread on at least one subject. It is that the "national state" (including democracies which can be meddlesome in their own right) must adopt a hands-off approach to regional cultures. A healthy regional culture does not need the state, that is, a "Federal Department of Education," a cradle-to-grave social security state, or other bureaucracies which only allow the national state to control its people. As such, regional cultures, as Weaver understood them, pose a grave threat to the power-hungry dreams of the centralized state. The national state wants consolidation of power and submission amongst its subjects. It will try through means fair or foul, to destroy stubborn regional cultures. For a softer approach, it will use economic "incentives" to "manipulate local officials...to reflect their will." In other words, if you let us (the "national state") take over your schools, we will give you loads of federal grants and monies. This tactic works particularly well in American public school districts.

Again, the battle Weaver's Confederate ancestors fought was never far from his mind. He declared more than once, that when the national state imposes its will on regional cultures, standards and morals are likely to take the "toboggan slide to vulgarity and obscenity." Regional cultures must say no to the national state or lose their identity as the push towards a drab and brutal uniformity continues.

A centralized government thus, is also distrustful of serious art. Weaver especially criticized the "Jacobism" practiced during the French Revolution and later by both Nazi Germany and Soviet Russia. Artists such as Ernest Hemingway present a portrait of man as a heroic figure who prefers the strenuous life to the dull conformity of the modern world. Like the discriminating individual that Weaver hoped the educational system would produce, the heroic figure will reject state coercion. Art, then, is a healthy form of rebellion. The twentieth-century artist—certainly in the case of T.S. Eliot and William Butler Yeats—is often a high reactionary. Eliot rejected the materialistic culture of the West and instead, worked to reconstruct a vision of Christendom. Yeats penned great mythologies celebrating the heroism of the Irish race. Both men created a metaphysical dream that transcended their corrupted age. In this essay, they were Weaver's prime examples of artists who sought to renew the culture of their adopted and native cultures.

With the rise of industrialism and urban culture, regional cultures, as Weaver oftentimes admitted, have been on the defensive. Technological advances in the form of television, movies, radio and videos, plus the enforcement of national educational "standards" have dealt one body blow after another to this vast nation's many colorful and distinct regional identities. A suburbanized America, with drab shopping malls and ugly highways running through "bedroom communities" (we commute to large cities for work and come home just in time to watch some television and then go to sleep) is the most obvious example of a non-descript national landscape.

And yet, those same regional cultures were the source of this nation's greatest creative outbursts. Weaver continually celebrated the "regional color" of American literature; here was a "diversity" worth saving. While New England civilization had some life left in it, Robert Frost used it as a locale for his distinctive poetic voice. The South resisted industrialism longer than other regions and so the "backward," benighted Dixie lived long enough in the past to produce the giants of early twentieth-century American literature. Meanwhile, the regions which had eagerly embraced the money-culture, the Midwest and Northeast, saw their most gifted sons—Hemingway, Eliot, Henry James, Ezra Pound, Glenway Wescott, F. Scott Fitzgerald—all flee to Europe to begin literary careers as determined and unapologetic expatriates.

So with society out of joint and culture on a downhill slide toward cheapness and vulgarity, how can regionalism survive? We fight destructive forces by defining regional cultures as "distinct, exclusive and autonomous." The controversial word is "exclusive." Weaver drops the term like a bomb; it jumps out and grabs the "sensitized" reader of the 1990s. To be sure, the term comes with qualifications; a culture is exclusive in that it must "maintain its own right to its own choices— its own inclusions and exclusions." No matter. There are, of course, problems with the term. In our time, "exclusive" qualifies as a major league devil term. The opposite of exclusive—inclusive—stands as a reigning god term, one used by politicians on both ends of the political spectrum. Furthermore, "exclusive" is hardly the language of progress. As Weaver noted in *The Southern Tradition at Bay*, the road back to the ethos of the Middle Ages or the Old South must be accompanied by progessive-sounding rhetoric: "The average man's metaphysic is summed up by this word; 'progressive' is his token of approval."[7]

Still, the logic of a culture maintaining its integrity by Weaver's definition of "exclusive" cannot be disputed. Religions, for example, are highly exclusive in their laws, customs, even their reading of history. No one would want followers of the Ayotollah Khomeini to storm the local church or synagogue and preach the new gospel. Weaver would apply the doctrine of exclusivity to other areas of culture. There is no need for multiculturalism to be taught to children in say, southern Indiana or western North Carolina. What's the point? These young people have already been born into a distinct culture. Let them learn its own unique history. A traditional society doesn't need new ideologies crashing its gates. It only needs to transmit its agreed-upon values and mythologies to the rising generation. Above all, a "distinct, exclusive and autonomous" culture is one that has mastery over its own destiny.[8]

Using such definitions is yet another example of Weaver's admirable boldness. We would never admit publicly that cultures are exclusive; privately, we hope the culture we are comfortable with endures. Emphasis on this polarizing term, then, adds greatly to the effectiveness of the essay.

The other strong points are the way Weaver defines culture as something necessary for man's well-being in a hostile world and as a phenomenon more satisfying than anything the political state can cook up. Weaver, in this essay, also declares he is all for pluralism and cultural diversity—at least within certain bounds. Even though he firmly believed that some cultures are superior to others (in a little dig at the Midwest where he spent most of his adult life, Weaver declared sixteenth-century France was more to his liking than modern-day Muncie, Indiana), Weaver was especially for differing cultures to flourish in their own way. He would not, for instance, want the cult of industrialism to wreak havoc on the remaining agrarian cultures of the "underdeveloped" world.

On the general subject of diversity, Weaver held one strong caveat. If one truly respects "diversity" then we must also recognize the autonomy of each of those different cultures. Anything else is just a fanatical attempt to destroy cultures (and the political state they create) which stand in the way of complete totalitarianism. Weaver is simply asking that we allow the right of each culture to flourish on its own terms and in times of crisis, to have the chance to renew itself.

6

The Nation's Stepchild:
The Southern Essays of Richard M. Weaver

Of course, Weaver could always direct conservatives to study the Southern tradition. From his perch in Chicago, the 20th century South still looked good to Richard Weaver. The Western world may have succumbed to materialism, but the South remained a bastion of Christendom, the region "conspicious in its resistance to [the] disintegration [of the modern world.]" In essays Weaver wrote about the South—collected by James J. Thompson and George M. Curtis II and published in a 1987 book, *The Southern Essays of Richard M. Weaver*— the prose is relaxed, mature, sometimes angry, but oftentimes, quite confident. In these essays we also see Weaver assuming the role played by the most unreconstructed of the postbellum apologists—Albert Taylor Bledsoe, Edwin Alderman, Henry Watterson—namely, that the South, bloodied, but unbowed; defeated, but unconquered; still mostly unreconstructed and unreconstructable, would rise to save the nation from fearsome global trends. Furthermore, its literature would teach a brash nation unschooled in tragedy lessons of human nature that could bring wisdom in times of crisis. Weaver was not alone in expressing these sentiments. His contemporaries, among them Andrew Lytle, Robert Penn Warren, and Walker Percy also expressed hope that the South with its love of tradition, its distrust of science and its wisdom gained from a tragic past might yet provide leaders similar in character to the men who made the American republic.[1]

Weaver might not have recognized much of twentieth-century

America, but he did recognize the South or at least *his* South, that is, the mountains and rural towns of western North Carolina, which in the 1940s and 1950s were not yet completely spoiled by the ravages of industrialism. However, there are also signs that Weaver knew the South was badly losing its agrarian inheritance. He spoke of a "good bit of betrayal from within" by Southern politicians and businessmen willing to be exploited by industrialists and capitalists. The idea of South Carolina becoming home to a hydrogen bomb project was an especial cause for gloom.

But such sentiments only surface sporadically. Although Weaver's Southern essays harken back to the antebellum and postbellum South, he is mostly defending the post-World War II South, which he still claimed—to borrow the title of a book Weaver contributed to—was the "enduring South." Writing about the modern South, Weaver is on familiar ground. While he saw the Western world in the stages of a moral and spiritual collapse that had been in progress for five centuries, he argued that the twentieth-century South still maintained much of the heritage described in *The Southern Tradition at Bay:* Namely, the older religiousness (which critics even back then dismissed as "fundamentalism"), a reverence for nature, piety, and a society that still had room for a hierarchy. For Weaver, the post-World War II South rejected the cult of massness.

Why was the South the nation's stepchild? There are all the popular stereotypes—the South was backward, bigoted, and rural. The South tended towards fundamentalism in a secular era. It was God-fearing in a nation defined by "success unlimited." The gaudy America of the twentieth century was a triumphant nation, a mighty empire that had seemingly transcended history. As Weaver writes in "The South And The American Union":

> The assumption is that the U.S. is somehow exempt from the past and present fate, as well as from many of the necessites, of other nations. Ours is a special creation, endowed with special immunities. As a kind of millennial state, it is not subject to the trials and divisions that have come upon others through time and history. History, it is commonly felt, consists of unpleasant things that happened to other people, and America bade goodbye to the sorrows along with the vices of the Old World.[2]

Then there is the Southern man. Continuing themes developed in *Ideas Have Consequences*, Weaver celebrated the common man, the yeoman farmer. The average Southerner is not a "victorious man."

Defeat and tragedy are part of his consciousness. He knows that "other men are living in a fool's paradise if they think man can never be defeated." He is not necessarily a prosperous man. He has known decades of poverty. He has seen his region defeated in wartime, occupied in defeat. He has seen his agrarian, Christian culture reconstructed by industrialists and proponents of evolution. Among all Americans, Southerners are alone in being told their heritage and history is an evil one; they have to change their ways before they can ever partake in the great American prosperity. Weaver even thought the old poverty was a blessing in disguise. Such "poverty" allowed Southerners to stay on the land and avoid the temptations of megalopolis.

How could the Southerner save the American household from destruction? Simply put, characteristics that made the South the "nation's stepchild" could also provide for that same nation's salvation. There was the older religiousness and fidelity to the "negative document." The Southerner, for one, was no leveller. He did not envy the man who achieved more or who accumulated more goods (as long as it was done honestly) than he. "Class war we neither have nor want," wrote one of Weaver's leading disciples, M.E. Bradford in the fiftieth anniversary sequel to *I'll Take My Stand*.[3] Recognizing the existence of original sin, evil, tragedy and man's fallibility, he also rejects attempts to perfect man through social engineering. The Southerner was willing to let distinctions and a hierarchy develop. Even into the twentieth century, Weaver felt enough of the Old South aristocracy existed to give hierarchy a good name. Always the defender of the gentlemanly class, Weaver assures us that "white-trash demagogues" such as Huey Long could never become the governor of Virginia.

The great Southern literature of the twentieth century, Weaver maintained, was the consequence of a region that treasured colorful rhetoric, anecdotal speech, and saw life as a great drama. In the Southerner's world view, culture, in this case, poetry, storytelling, and dramatic rhetoric was more important than economics. But in the wider Western world, a secular belief that the state could save us dominated the political culture. And so the South was exactly the inward-looking culture that would resist state control; in short, it was an example of the healthy cultures Weaver defined in "The Importance of Cultural Freedom."

Despite its inwardness, Weaver also predicted the South would play a decisive role in the great global conflicts of the twentieth century. It was the American South, the conservative region that cherished personality over abstractions which emerged as the nation's greatest opponent of fascism and communism. His brilliant essay, "The South and the Revolution of Nihilism" explains why the South played a major role in America's triumph over fascism. The military arts tradition was important, so was the willingness to fight and die for a metaphysical dream of the world.

> The South, by its firm grasp of the traditions of our civilization, has had a great part in giving us one more chance for the conservative solution. While the old sources of power and self-confidence were being weakened by debunking and scientific investigation, it clung to the belief that man is not saved by science alone, that myths and sentiments are part of the constitution of a nation, and that poetry ultimately decides more issues than economics. In the choice that had to be made its voice was perhaps decisive; and the choice was betwen a world illuminated by religious and poetical concepts and made human by respect for personality, and a world of materalism and technology, of an ever greater feeding of the physical man, which is nihilism.[4]

Southern Politics

Two essays, one examining the differences between the nineteenth-century Virginia senator, John Randolph of Roanoke and Henry David Thoreau, and the other comparing Daniel Webster to the less well-known South Carolina senator, Robert Young Hayne, were to be chapters in a book Weaver was writing at the time of his death. The book would compare other Southerners and New Englanders, and according to Bradford would be "an American Plutarch contrasting exemplary Southern and Northern types; a collection of papers on American rhetorical landmarks; a study of conflict in the American churches over slavery; and a few other items reaching out toward a transregional definition of the national character." Taking these two as an example, the book, if completed, would have been a devastating portrait, favorably comparing the virtues of Southern men who understood man's dual nature to those who erroneously followed Emerson's later belief in man's eternal goodness.[5]

The Southern political tradition was animated by complete fidelity to the U.S. Constitution. It stood against any would-be American empire and vigorously opposed expanding the powers of the centralized state. However, the same tradition did not promote anarchy. It called for a small government that would simply allow the people (in the nineteenth-century term, this meant the farmer and craftsmen in various professions) to live normal lives. The state, Weaver makes clear, worked best when it was closer to home. A county seat, a state government was far more effective in preserving constitutional government than the far-off government in Washington, D.C. A national government had its duties, but like many of their New England brethren, Southern conservatives wanted to keep its powers at arm's length. This is an idea which has fallen in and out of favor throughout the nation's history.

John Randolph of Roanoke, like Richard Weaver, remains a hero to the Old Right. Randolph's iconic status was established by Russell Kirk's 1951 monograph on the Virginian, a study that preceded Kirk's more famous *The Conservative Mind*. A famous Randolph statement— "I am an aristocrat. I hate equality, I love liberty"—has always been a guiding force for conservatives who believe that any government-enforced "equality" destroys the laws of merit and reward. Many years later, when remnants of the Old Right saw their movement threatened by a dominant neoconservatism that still championed the statism of the New Deal, the "paleoconservatives" formed the John Randolph Society, bringing traditionalists and libertarians into a political union that was given a publicity boost by the presidential campaigns of fellow society member Patrick Buchanan. Many of the members were affiliated with the Rockford Institute in Rockford, Illinois, which publishes the Old Right flagship publication, *Chronicles* and annually awards the Richard M. Weaver Award for Scholarly Letters.

The comparison between Randolph and Thoreau in "Two Types of American Individualism," (also collected in *Life Without Prejudice*) is so devastating that one may forget Weaver admired Thoreau's writing skills, the former's attacks on the Leviathan state, and his independent spirit. Thoreau was the quintessential American individualist, a man perfectly willing to live without the welfare state. He was also an agrarian, someone well practiced in the art of subsistence farming. But the more famous New Englander (in all cases, the New Englander is more famous in American lore) is also dissected as a "philosopher on holiday" who wishes to escape the drama of the real world. Thoreau, for instance, refused to pay a church levy which in turn pays for the schools and other institutions that educated and nurtured him. When the Civil War broke out, Thoreau did not become involved in any civilian capacity (he was in his forties already). Instead, he told a friend to ignore the coming war. Such inaction would be "the most fatal . . . weapon you can direct against evil." On the question of slavery, Thoreau dutifully signed up for the abolitionist movement, but never offered any idea or plan as to what might be done to help the freed slaves. Thoreau can be characterized as representing an extreme version of libertarianism. With him the state was "nowhere to be seen." To Weaver, this was an attitude that was both egotistical and irresponsible.[6]

Randolph, on the other hand, typified a "social bond individualism." He was an aristocrat from the Old Southern school, a political animal who started out as a strong states' rights man and never wavered one iota from the cause. No fire-breather, Randolph sought compromises in the secession crises of both 1812–1814 (when New England threatened to secede over the War of 1812) and 1832 (when South Carolina was unhappy with new tariff laws). In the first instance, he sought out Speaker of the House Henry Clay to broker a compromise. His reasoning in 1814 was that while the New England states certainly had the constitutional right to secede, their general welfare was better served by staying in a potentially prosperous union.

Like Jefferson and Washington, Randolph opposed slavery. And also like his fellow Virginians, he provided for his slaves well-being once they were freed. Each of Randolph's former slaves over age forty were given ten acres of land to begin their new lives. To Weaver, this contrasts markedly with Thoreau's apparent belief that emancipation would cause no problems to either whites or blacks. But when the question of slavery arose in Missouri, Randolph stuck with the Constitution, declaring that that document allowed Missouri to enter the Union as either a slave or free state.

In all his actions, Randolph lived up to the education of the gentleman. He was part of his community's social and political life. Rather than withdrawing from society, "[his] tactic in dealing with an evil was to hold it up in all its repulsiveness and then urge that something be done to overcome it." He admirably lived up to Weaver's belief that a man must seek more than personal gratification in life. Weaver identified Randolph's conservatism as being firmly rooted in the Christian tradition: it was antimillenial and preferred persuasion and reform to a revolutionary creed that Weaver deemed anti-Christian. Randolph's social bond individualism is a guide to regaining true individualism and personality in a world overrun by busybody collectivists. It was civil (he urged compromise and reconciliation in times of crisis), viable (his politics operated strictly within the confines of the constitution), and considerate. Thoreau, on the other hand, had a bad habit of withdrawing from society.[7]

Like Randolph, Robert Young Hayne had a "Southern vision" of politics that Weaver found agreeable. The senator opposed the idea of an American empire. An early nineteenth-century debate over what to do with unsold federal lands inspired Weaver's "Two Orators," an essay about the Senate debate that dramatized the competing visions of America's destiny. Senator Daniel Webster of New Hampshire wanted the land sold; Senator Hayne of South Carolina opposed the sale.

Webster was the opposite of Thoreau. While the latter was a dropout from society, Webster moved to grab the controls of the soon-to-be all powerful centralized government. He was also a man with a vision. The land sale was a step toward something larger. Webster saw America evolving into a grand empire, "diffusing light and blessings throughout the world." Thus he was a forerunner of the Manifest Destiny of the Polk era, the "splendid little war" of 1898, a world war to make the world safe for democracy to finally, the "New World Order" and "nation building" of the 1990s.

Webster's position also represented a great shift in the New England mind. New Englanders, we recall, were as jealous in their defense of states' rights as any fire-breather from South Carolina; indeed, we have already seen the region's desire to secede during the War of 1812. Weaver explains Webster's changing philosophy as due partly to personal ambition. One of the great figures in American history, Webster's fame rests on oratory and literary achievements. But as with many legislative giants, Webster sought the presidency. As he aged, the great prize seemed to be slipping away. Hence the evolution from the New England tradition of regionalism to dreams of empire.

In addition to opposing the idea of Manifest Destiny, Hayne enunciated familiar conservative principles of limited government when opposing the sale of federal lands. He opposed any debt the sale might cause. Accumulation of debt would increase the size of government. A bloated government only increases the public's dependency on the state. Increased dependency, in turn, means less individual freedom. To use dependency as a social bond was a "base interest . . . opposed to the principle of free government and at war with virtue and patriotism."

For Weaver, Senator Hayne's sentiments reflected the South's feudal tradition and her preference for localism over centralism. Senator Hayne was not an orator seeking to remake the world in America's image. He wanted to defend the constitution from "enthusiastic visions" of power and glory harbored by Webster. Hayne concurred with Randolph's view of government as a "wise and masterly inactivity," insuring stability and local rule.[8]

To be sure, the philosophy of both Randolph and Hayne was not always the dominant strain in Southern political thought. Thomas Jefferson could be excused for the Louisiana Purchase; that large chunk of land was there for the taking and Jefferson harbored no imperial ambitions. The Louisiana Purchase did not cost any American blood nor was it a cause of tension between the North and South. However, the Mexican War was a different story. This conflict extended the nation's territory well past the Mississippi River. The balance of power between North and South was upset for good, which is why John C. Calhoun, a former war hawk, strongly opposed Mr. Polk's war. The Spanish-American War took the American empire into the Caribbean and the Far East, while World War I finished the job, transforming the U.S. into a full-fledged global power. Even Weaver's Confederacy might not have been immune from the itch. Such a learned observer as Andrew Lytle has acknowledged that a victorious Confederacy (now even more confident of its military prowess) probably would have taken on the declining Spanish Empire in Mexico and Cuba. The mid-to-late nineteenth century was a time of empire and the newly industrialized America had no desire to stay on the sidelines.

Randolph represented the polar opposite of Polk or Woodrow Wilson. He even opposed the Louisiana Purchase by declaring his fidelity to "the old 13." Likewise, Randolph had little use for the culture of the Wild West, preferring, instead, the social classes which defined the Old South. For both Hayne and Randolph, the Constitution came first. They read nothing "relevant" into its lines. Local rule even more than "states' rights" was paramount. Both were "small r" republicans and public servants in the true sense of the word. Their concerns remained with the landowners back home, not the commercial benefits of an expanding empire.

Although he isn't remembered as a great orator, Senator Hayne took the Southern tradition beyond a mere reading of the Constitution. Weaver's essay certainly amounts to a solid defense of federalism. But

Senator Hayne also presented a brilliant metaphysical vision of a reponsible government. Freedom was a condition for men to enjoy. A man finds happiness in his place of habitation, in the regional culture that nurtures him and shapes his thinking. Weaver used words such as "happiness," "contentment," and "sentiment" to describe the state of a stable community. And he left no doubt that a wise and masterly government plays a major role in such a development.

At times, this sounds almost utopian, as if the state can create civil communities populated by happy men and women. Perhaps these are remnants of Weaver's old flirtation with socialism. Local rule, indeed, can be as corrupt as the centralized state. Once again, it all comes down to virtue. And Weaver left no doubt that the nineteenth-century American, the rural man, was far more virtuous, far more fit for the responsibilities of freedom than his twentieth-century successor who wallowed in the abyss of megalopolis and was utterly dependent on the Leviathan state for his economic survival.

An exception was the American South. A major theme of *The Southern Essays* is Weaver's intention to defend the 1950s South from meddlesome outsiders. As the second reconstruction geared into full swing, Weaver's place was not to criticize the South—he saw its faults, but they were minor next to the region's virtues. Instead, he defended the South against "the forces of planned disintegration"; especially judges and legislators all raining down edicts from afar. By championing Randolph and Hayne, Weaver gave the modern South political philosophers to serve as models for present-day battles. He also meant to show that the South remained true to the decentralizing tenets of the constitution while New Englanders had become coercive utopians determined to remake the world in their own egalitarian vision.

Southern Literature

The nineteenth-century South's great contribution to the nation was in politics, as soldier/statesmen such as George Washington, Andrew Jackson, and Zachary Taylor and political theorists Thomas Jefferson, John C. Calhoun, John Randolph of Roanoke all helped to shape the American republic. However, when General Lee turned over his sword to General Grant, the South's era of political clout in America, at least for a good five decades, came crashing to a halt. Henceforth, her sons and daughters took up the pen, at first to apologize for the old regime but then more successfully to write a great, timeless literature that examined the ancient questions of human nature. If during the nineteenth century, the South had made its mark on history through political theory, in the twentieth century, literature was the region's gift to America.

Even more inspiring than Weaver's defense of the South's political traditions was his celebration of Southern literature. By the 1920s, Southern writers were beginning to mature. They had moved away from the sentimentality of Thomas Nelson Page or the cynicism of Ellen Glasgow to something more profound. For Allen Tate, the change came after World War I. The South would enter the modern world, but in doing so, the region's writers would also take a "glance backward" to its tragic past. Tate also noticed that the South, "looked around and saw for the first time since 1830 that the Yankees were not to blame for everything . . . the Southern legend . . . of defeat and heroic frustration was taken over by a dozen or more first-rate writers and converted into a universal myth of the human condition."[9]

By the 1950s, the Southern Renaissance seemed triumphant. The nation, and indeed the world, came to honor the achievement of Southern literature. At the beginning of the decade, William Faulkner was awarded the Nobel Prize for Literature and the South's preeminence in fiction, poetry, and criticism was, for a brief moment in the nation's literary history, unquestioned. In addition to Faulkner, Weaver's Agraraian mentors, especially Tate, John Crowe Ransom, Robert Penn Warren, Cleanth Brooks, and Andrew Lytle had all secured positions as prime makers of modern literature. The New Criticism, championed by Ransom, Tate, Brooks, and Warren—most spectacularly in the success of the latter two's famous textbook *Understanding Poetry*—exerted great influence throughout the English-speaking world. In addition, female novelists such as Caroline Gordon, Flannery O'Connor, Eudora Welty, and Katherine Ann Porter were considered essential reading for any serious student of American literature.

Why did the South dominate American letters? For one, Southerners were highly "mythopoetic," that is, they relished the power of mythology. The American tall tale, Weaver recalled, was invented by Southerners. The great mythological images of American civilization— George Washington and the cherry tree, Daniel Boone and the wild frontier, Davey Crockett fighting at the Alamo, Stonewall Jackson standing tall at Manassas, even General George S. Patton emphasized his Southern roots—were all Southern in their origin. Of course, not all American mythology is Southern; there is Ben Franklin's rise to prosperity and Paul Revere's midnight ride through Boston. However, the South's love of mythology lasted well into the twentieth century when there was little time for storytelling in our hectic daily lives. Notes Weaver:

> I have heard people ask where William Faulkner gets that stuff that goes into his novels—whether he dreams it in nightmares, and so on. No one who had spent any time in Mississippi with his ear open would have to ask that question. He would know to what extent incidents and stories of this kind enter into the imaginative life of Mississippians. This mythopoeic or poetic—in the Aristotelian sense—faculty is surely behind the present flowering of the Southern novel and short story. It has already given us an interesting body of fiction and it may one day give us a great literature. The South is not so much sleeping as dreaming, and dreams sometimes begat creations![10]

In 1958, Vanderbilt University hosted a conference on Southern literature. Weaver was invited to speak and he delivered a paper, later published as "Contemporary Southern Literature." Weaver favorably compared Southern literature to other regional products. The mind of New England, following the example of Emerson, had now declared man to be a naturally good being, a disastrous presumption that was strong enough to "blow up any society [on] which it is founded."

Midwestern literature, at least in the novels of Theodore Dreiser and Frank Norris, took a different, more gloomy view: Man was a victim of circumstances, he was a peon, a serf, his individualism trampled down by the mighty forces of industrialism. Such a message packed a powerful punch, but it wasn't enough to explain the entire human condition. Man has to be portrayed as something more than a victim: it was more honest, Weaver felt, to show that he has a hand in controlling his own destiny.

Southern literature, on the other hand, was grounded firmly in the Western tradition. Its predecessors were found in the classics of ancient Athens, Rome, and Elizabethan England. To Richard Weaver, Southern literature, above all, presented the correct dual view of man's nature. The novels of Faulkner, Warren, Thomas Wolfe, and Jesse Stuart; the poetry of Ransom, Warren, Tate, and Davidson all showed "man in his passion." Here also was man being depicted as a monster, an angel, a hero, a villain. This literature also displayed great piety towards a tragic past expressed through a high, colorful rhetoric. Furthermore, Southern

writers understood—as T.S. Eliot once put it—man's capacity for both
damnation and salvation. As such, they viewed our life's experiences,
our struggles, trials, triumphs, and tragedies as something momentous.
Man is not a helpless victim or a naturally good angel. In the classical-
Christian tradition, he is a creature of free choice.

That Southern literature was animated by tragedy is not an original
view, but Weaver illuminates with his own considerable subtlety. Tragedy, Weaver writes, means man must choose between good and evil.
Such a choice (and the fact that man will often make the wrong choice)
confirms the South's "Christian point of view" that man can fall. The
South, also, was "the region history happened to." This means remem-
bering the region's triumphs—its role in winning the Revolutionary
War, producing statesmen such as Washington, Jefferson, Patrick Henry,
and, in general, building a civilization that had the spirit to defeat the
world's greatest empire.

As significant, however, is the South's tragic past. America remains
(notoriously for some) an incorrigbly optimistic nation. In *Ideas Have
Consequences*, for instance, Weaver railed against this "hysterical optimism" which prevented Americans from understanding man's fragility, his weaknesses, and "the immemorial tendency of man to do the
wrong thing when he knows the right thing." Tragedy isn't considered
a part of our unfolding American pageantry. The Civil War, reconstruction, military occupation, scalawag legislators, the decades of poverty, the feeling for decades that the region was no longer part of a
prosperous nation—that is the stuff of great tragedy and it provided
the South with "probably the most deeply educational experience" a
people can have. The defeated, impoverished South was very real in
the lives of the the young Faulkner, Lytle, Warren, Donald Davidson
and other giants of the Southern Renaissance.

Not only the existence of tragedy, but the presence of evil also
inspired Southern literature. That man can be monstrous is obvious to
a somber observer of life, but in an age that celebrated the goodness of
man, the acknowledgment of the monstrous added a special validity to
the South's literature; by signifying the existence of original sin. Most
notable to Weaver was Lilburn Lewis, nephew to Thomas Jefferson,
who in Warren's *Brother to Dragons*, savagely murders a slave, shock-
ing his famous uncle and mocking Jefferson's earlier belief in the
natural goodness of man. One could add Faulkner's most famous "monster," Thomas Sutpen. A poor white from Virginia, Sutpen dreams of

glory in Mississippi, operating "Sutpen's 100" (a large plantation) and building his own financial empire in the Magnolia State. A man of great bravery, wealth, and ambition, Sutpen's virtues, were to Cleanth Brooks, "those of the typical twentieth-century man." As were his vices, "his dismissal of the past, his commitment to the future, and his confidence that, with courage and know-how, he can accomplish literally anything." Monsters existed in the literature of ancient Greece and Rome and in the plays of Shakespeare. That they also existed in Southern literature was a testimony to "an honest artistic vision."[11]

Not all of Southern literature is so gloomy. The world that has tragedy, monsters, and sinners will also have heroes lest it perish completely. Characters in Southern novels and poems were not passive bystanders to history. They jumped into life's experiences. Thomas Wolfe is the model here as Weaver pays homage to his fellow Tar Heel. Wolfe's autobiographical hero, Eugene Gant goes through life "as a modern Gargantua with a monstrous appetite for experience." The Agrarians did not see Wolfe as part of the Southern tradition. Wolfe's own background was "mixed," his father wandered South from Pennsylvania and voted the straight Republican line at a time when the only Republicans in the South were transplanted Northerners like W.O. Wolfe. Thomas Wolfe rarely identified himself as a Southern writer. Instead, his theme was "America" itself, something far more wide-ranging and at times, more abstract than the provincialism of Faulkner or Eudora Welty.

But for Weaver, the larger-than-life characters in Wolfe's fiction, plus the novelist's colorful rhetoric, was an important element of Southern fiction. There are other examples. Characters from Faulkner and Warren "are heroes of a long odyssey of experience surviving many clashes with environments and people"; poems by Allen Tate and John Crowe Ransom which memorialized Confederate heroes and the South as "a land where heroes stood 'and drenched it with their only blood.'"[12]

These artists not only celebrate human valor but offer a stunning antidote to the dreary ideologies of the century. The hero, as Weaver maintained throughout his writings, is the man who stands apart from the crowd. He is a figure of courage and action who refuses to succumb to "servile emotions." By celebrating this brand of heroism, Southern writers challenged the Marxist attempt to "de-individualize" man, to submerge him into the masses, to make him dependent on the state to the point where he can never liberate himself. Southern writers weren't the only modern-day literary figures who opposed the cult of massness, but the use of high and colorful rhetoric in the novels of Faulkner, Warren and Wolfe elevated their revolution to more dramatic heights.

The train of history that rolled over the South inspired much of its literature. But the fact that the region remained a traditional society in its manners, morals, and codes of conduct also loomed large in creating a mature arts and letters. When certain customs are established, then a language develops. Rhetoric played a key role in Weaver's celebration of Southern literature. The world of monsters and heroes was magnified by a colorful language with an emphasis on rhetorical flourish—the same spaciousness that Weaver so admired in the political rhetoric of the early America.

A great novelist such as Ernest Hemingway also created his own style, his own use of the language. But Hemingway's prose—and Weaver admired Hemingway's heroes as men who stood apart from the crowd—does not soar to the levels of Faulkner or Wolfe. I am reminded of a comparison I read years ago by Bruce McElderry of death scenes in Hemingway's *A Farewell to Arms* and Wolfe's *Look Homeward, Angel.* First there is Hemingway's bleak prose that summed up Lieutenant Henry's feelings about the dead mother of his dead child: "It was like saying goodbye to a statue. After a while I went out and left the hospital and walked back to the hotel in the rain." And then there is the death of Ben Gant, Eugene Gant's favorite brother. Wolfe's lyricism in describing the death scene couldn't provide a more vivid contrast in styles:

Filled with a terrible vision of all life in the one moment, he seemed to rise forward bodilessly from his pillows without support—a flame, a light, a glory—joined at length in death to the dark spirit who had brooded upon each footstep of his lonely adventure on earth; and, casting the fierce sword of his glance with utter and final comprehension upon the room haunted with its gray pageantry of cheap loves and dull consciences and on all those uncertain murmers of waste and confusion fading now from the bright window of his eyes, he passed instantly, scornful and unafraid, as he had lived, into the shades of death.

We can believe in the nothingness of life, we can believe in the nothingness of death and of life after death—but who can believe in the nothingness of Ben? Like Apollo, who did his penance to the high god in the sad house of King Admetus, he came, a god with broken feet, into the gray hovel of this world. And he lived here a stranger, trying to recapture the music of the lost world, trying to recall the great forgotten language, the lost faces, the stone, the leaf, the door.

O Artemidorus, farewell![13]

In *A Farewell to Arms*, it is as if the mother and child had never existed. Lieutenant Henry is saying goodbye to "statues," not dead human beings. But Eugene's brother Ben is both mourned and celebrated as an epic figure. Ben went through life as a frustrated newspaperman who could not escape his generally unhappy existence. But he also served as a best friend and mentor to his confused younger brother. He was a selfless hero, guiding Eugene through adolescence and early adulthood. Ben Gant emerges, then as a tragic hero whose life had great significance. Or as McElderry describes the death scene: "There is no numbness here. In the presence of death, there is a vibrant sense of life." And a tradition that honors the drama and significance of the human experience.[14]

As with the postbellum apologists, Weaver saw lofty prospects for the legacy of the Southern Renaissance. Indeed, he hoped it might shake the nation with the same mighty force once reserved for the South's political traditions. Southern literature was aesthetically pleasing; through themes of tragedy and heroism, it told us something important and timely about the human condition. Such themes also taught essential lessons about man's limitations: he can't conquer nature, no amount of social engineering will change his behavior, he is a sinner, a saint, a monster, an angel. Such lessons, Weaver hoped, would be a liberating experience for a nation that was embracing salvation through state measures.

> Here is the chief glory and continuing mission of Southern literature. It holds up an image of man which is derived not from some partial philosophical system, but from observation, history, traditional beliefs older than any "ism," and from the final artistic apperception. The fact that this image seems to be capturing the imagination of the country may be a sign that we are girding ourselves inwardly for the struggle against those haters of humanity and despisers of all human affections who today control a good part of the world. Those who capture the imagination of the country are, no matter how unofficially, in a position of leadership. The South, which has spent so many years as America's stepchild, is proving to have the gift which may save the household from destruction.[15]

The Agrarians: Their Rise and Fall

Several chapters in *The Southern Essays* are homages to the Tennessee Agrarians (this is Weaver's term, elsewhere they are referred to as the Vanderbilt Agrarians or the Southern Agrarians). The Agrarians, were of course, main players in the Southern Renaissance. "[Without] the Agrarians, the [Southern] Renaissance is not intelligble," M.E. Bradford has correctly stated. Their essays and poems contemplated the importance of religion to sustaining a traditional society. In the case of Donald Davidson and Andrew Lytle, there was also a robust celebration of the folkways that flourished in the Middle South. But their mission was much different from other Southern writers. The Agrarians affirmed the humane tradition of a rural society, but they also juxtaposed it with a scorching critique of industrialism.

For Weaver, the significance of the Agrarians could never be underestimated. They represented nothing less than the first Southern offensive against the forces of planned disintegration since the bold manuevers by Lee and Jackson in the early 1860s. While Faulkner and Wolfe went their own ways (both lived in Europe and Greenwich Village; Faulkner returned to the South, while Wolfe stayed in New York City), the Agrarians came together, first as poets at Vanderbilt, then as writers determined to defend the South's Christian inheritance. *I'll Take My Stand,* Weaver noted, was the product of men who shared the same heritage, traditions, and vocation. As poets, Ransom, Warren, Tate, and Davidson, were, before the rest of us, able to foresee the destructive effects of industrialism. They were able to explain what was wrong with an industrial/urban culture and what was right and good about the old ways. Weaver correctly notes that his old mentor, John Crowe Ransom never wrote better or with more insight than when he addressed the crisis of industrialism. Here he cites a famous Ransom passage on the same subject.

> Progress never defines its ultimate objective but thrusts its victims at once into an infinite series. Our vast industrial machine, with its laboratory center of experimentation, and its far-flung organs of mass production, is like a Prussianized state which is organized strictly for war and can never consent to peace. . . . Industrialism is rightfully a menial, of almost miraculous cunning, but no intelligence; it needs to be strongly governed, or it will destroy the economy of the household. Only a community of tough conservative habit can master it.[16]

And there is Ransom's defense of the old ways.

> The good life depends on leisure, but leisure depends on an establishment—and the establishment depends on a prevailing magnanimity which scorns personal advancement at the expense of the free activity of the mind.[17]

An industrial society, like a Marxist one, would do away with individualism and create the vaunted "mass man." This is all right, progressives reasoned, because like the Marxist regime, industrialism would create economic prosperity, resulting in harmonius living and social progress. Industrialism does not defend a traditional society. It too wants to create a "new" man. The new world, built by science and defined by progress, will make history's stern lessons obsolete.

The Agrarians drilled holes into all this nonsense. They were also able to say why farming was man's "best vocation." Weaver cited Aristotle who considered farmers the "best common people." Because they were hard-working property owners with little time for frivolity and no desire to "covet their neighbors goods," farmers were virtuous citizens, those most capable of sustaining a vital democracy—a fact not lost on Thomas Jefferson many centuries later. In all, the Agrarians represented a "complete regime." They celebrated the joys of rural living, the pleasure one finds from a vital folk art culture. The Agrarians also attacked the bland collectivism of an industrial society, the "brutal and hurried" regimentation of work and daily life, the high unemployement and lack of job security this new economy actually brings.

Because they were poets and novelists, Ransom, Tate, Davidson, and Lytle all made a more lyrical defense of an agrarian society than Weaver, for the most part, was capable of providing (the life of the Vermont farmer in *Ideas* is an exception). Lytle's description of Middle Tennessee farm life in "The Hind Tit," for instance, is unmatched in American literature. Not that Weaver wasn't convincing, but his defense of agrarianism in *Ideas Have Consequences* was launched in the midst of an angry attack on urban culture. The Agrarians did not take their stand as exiles. None of them wrote a jeremiad as brilliant as *Ideas*, but since they, at least at first, stayed close to home, a pleasing vision of agrarian life shines through more strongly in their essays.

These differences are merely a matter of style. Weaver and the Agrarians both viewed work as something productive and pleasing, a condition they agreed was more likely to occur in a pastoral community. An agrarian culture also found time for the development of the folk arts. In households all across the early American republic, the fiddle was considered the most valuable piece of furniture. As importantly, "such practices as manners, conversation, hospitality, sympathy, family life, romantic love," all of which "reveal and develop sensibility in human affairs" were destroyed in the maddening tempo of the industrial world, but stayed intact in an agrarian community.[18]

The Agrarians were also the foremost Jeffersonians of their day. Their ancestors had fought in the two great conflicts of American history, the Revolutionary War and the Civil War. American history was, as Robert Penn Warren put it, a "felt history" to the Agrarians, not just something barely mentioned in public school textbooks. They shared Jefferson's vision of small landowners constituting the backbone of American liberty. The Agrarians—especially Lytle and Davidson—knew what the Founding Fathers envisioned for America, they also bitterly acknowledged in essays and poems, how the centralized state and forces of industrialism ruined the Old Republic. Both Weaver and the Agrarians continually celebrated the same nonmaterialistic society that was the South's great gift to the modern world.

Furthermore, Agrarianism, to Weaver, was a superior philosophy to the competing ideologies of the 1930s; primarily those of Humanism, Marxism, and the New Deal.

> Humanism was very much a cult, not only unable to propagate itself generally but also unable to win stocktakers among the intellectuals for very long. Marxism was fatally flawed by its assumption that economics is the prime determinant of social organization. Technocracy was nothing more than an engineering approach to the problems of economic dislocation. New Dealism, though socialistic in tendency, hardly enjoyed the benefits of a theory at all; it was a hand-to-mouth dealing with problems created by the Great Depression, a set of improvisations which became more politicized as time went on.[19]

Weaver also noticed that *I'll Take My Stand,* because it showed the South acting *in character*, (italics are Weaver's) was well received in the North. But Southern reviewers were mostly hostile. Years later, a frustrated Donald Davidson remarked that *I'll Stand My Stand* became one of those books discussed with authority by people who never bothered plowing through its pages. "[*I'll Take My Stand*] has this unique distinction," he claimed, "it has been refuted by more people who have never read it—or even seen a copy—than any other book in American history." Responding to Davidson's bitterness, Allen Tate tried to console his friend by declaring that the brief movement had its lasting effects. "You eventually believe that agrarianism was a failure," Tate wrote Davidson, "I think it was and is a very great success;

but then I never expected it to have any political influence. It is a reaffirmation of the humane tradition, and to reaffirm that is an end in itself. Never fear; we shall be remembered when our snipers are forgotten."[20]

But Weaver, like Davidson, envisioned the book as a springboard for political success:

> Undoubtedly, the Agrarians would exert an immensely greater influence if they held some city or some university, if they had a concentration of forces which would serve as a radiating center of impulse—if they had a Rome, as it were.[21]

It never happened. The New South steamroller broke up the Agrarian fraternity. There was a time when Ransom shared Davidson's desire for political success. In *I'll Take My Stand*, Ransom hoped for a political coalition of freedom-loving, individualistic Southerners and Westerners to combat the Leviathan state. Ransom even defended the Agrarian cause in a series of public debates with Southern liberals. But by the late 1930s, Ransom became disillusioned with the whole faltering movement, eventually declaring that limited forms of industrialism were acceptable.

More importantly, the administration at Vanderbilt had no use for Agrarianism. The young Robert Penn Warren was denied even a night teaching job at a local college by the head of the Vanderbilt English Department. And when Ransom was offered a position at Kenyon College in Ohio, the Vanderbilt hierarchy, to the astonishment of the literary world, made no great effort to keep him. That just about did it. At Kenyon, Ransom concentrated on literary criticism and building up the influential *Kenyon Review*, but an Agrarian movement built around faculty members at Vanderbilt was over. As such, Davidson, who never retreated from his Agrarian convictions, suffered in his isolation. The Vanderbilt faculty increasingly viewed him as an anachronism, even an embarrassment. Davidson's stand against federal public school desegregation orders caused him further alienation. For relief, he would take a summer position at Robert Frost's Bread Loaf writing school in Vermont.[22]

Weaver himself seemed embittered by the movement's political failure. In "The Southern Phoenix," he noticed that some of the charter Agrarians no longer suscribed to their original positions (he certainly had Ransom in mind, but would never say so publicly). Weaver waxed philosophical: people can become bored "with an idea," there are personal considerations, instances of indifference, estrangement (one can leave the South) or "one can simply grow old." Worse yet, the Southern people failed to heed the poet's warnings. Andrew Lytle liked to recall that when *I'll Take My Stand* first appeared, Southerners were sympathetic but not alarmed: they assumed their way of life would endure. Weaver claimed, somewhat bitterly, that the Agrarians "saw their compatriots turn away in large numbers from their recommendations." As such, the Agrarians were like John Milton who authored *A Ready and Easy Way to Establish A Free Commonwealth* just as Englishmen were welcoming the restored monarchy of Charles II. Both Milton and the Agrarians, Weaver reasoned, were condemned to the biblical fate all homegrown prophets must suffer.[23]

In "Agrarianism In Exile," Weaver later suggested that the dispersal of Southern traditionalists to Northern universities might help them find allies in their continuing struggle. However, the presence of Warren and Cleanth Brooks at Yale, Tate at Minnesota, Ransom at Kenyon—or Weaver at Chicago—hardly convinced liberals who dominated those universities that Agrarianism was a cause worth joining.

Needless to say, much has changed since Weaver wrote these essays in the 1950s. Even reading them is bit like going through a time warp. Social changes (desegregation, voting rights, etc.) are obvious, but so is the New South of sprawling urban areas dotting the region from Richmond to Houston. A prosperity unimagined by Weaver has taken hold, but with the rise of the Sunbelt South has also come, in many places, the same overwhelming urban culture he first attacked in *The Southern Tradition at Bay* and *Ideas Have Consequences*. Now, the problems of Atlanta, New Orleans, Birmingham, Memphis, Dallas, Houston, and other cities have become practically indistinguishable from those in New York City, Los Angeles, Chicago, Detroit, Philadelphia and other centers of the dreaded megalopolis. Since 1975, over three million Americans have moved into the states of the Old Confederacy. And there is this paradox: as the South grows in population (and political clout), the real South seems to be shrinking daily. Florida, Northern Virginia, the Atlanta area, Houston, Dallas, Charlotte, Raleigh-Durham—is it the traditional South or just a Los Angeles-style culture springing up all over Dixie?

The spread of industrialism in the South surprised even the most foreboding of the Agrarian philosophers. Fred Hobson imagined that if Weaver had witnessed the rise of the Sunbelt South, "he would have questioned, rightly so, whether the new superior South, confident and optimistic, possessed the discipline and integrity of the old." Weaver might have also asked if the industrialized South had any control over its economic destiny. After all, if an industrialist moves South in search of cheap, non-union labor, he will just as easily in the future move elsewhere in search of even cheaper help. And what is left are families, towns, and villages devastated by the effects of economic imperialism.[24]

The political scene is also in flux. From the late 1960s onward, the South has become the major battlefield in American politics. The Democratic Solid South did its duty throughout most of the twentieth century. The South was enthusiastic for the New Deal, but President Roosevelt's "court-packing" plan for the Supreme Court and other excesses created a coalition of Southern Democrats and Republicans that kept the New Deal revolution confined mostly to welfare-state politics, which the middle class, as the chief beneficiaries, then accepted. However, the push for federal civil rights and voting rights laws, plus the catacylsmic *Brown vs. Board* Supreme Court ruling began the unravelling of the Democratic South. By the early 1970s, the realignment from a Democratic to Republican South was well in motion.

Today, the Republican party has triumphed, but as John Shelton Reed once put it, it's not the same old stand anymore. Consider the Republican party leadership. The House speaker is a Southerner, but Newt Gingrich has nothing in common with such famous Georgians of the old Democratic era, for instance Richard Russell and Walter George. Gingrich is an enthusiastic technocrat (he fantasizes about providing a laptop computer for every schoolkid), a man firmly convinced technology can save us. He is a disciple of Alvin Toffler, the futurist who considers the agrarian world old hat, something outdated; an era whose passing we need not mourn. Gingrich also represents a booming Atlanta suburban district where many, if not most, of the residents are, like the speaker, transplanted Northerners who like the low-tax, low-mortgage Sunbelt.

Indeed, optimism about the South today is almost exclusively based on economic prosperity. Businessmen, corporate CEOs, and industrialists all like the South's low-wage, non-union workforce. But some things haven't changed. On the edge of the millennium, the South can still lay claim as the Western world's last redoubt of Christendom.

Economic boosterism now co-exists uneasily with a rising grass-roots, traditionalist-oriented movement (the "religious right") which feels threatened by an ever-advancing industrial/technological society. People can afford cable television and VCR's—but can they protect their children from what comes out of these contraptions?

As it long ago accepted goodies from a centralized government (i.e., public schools), the South is hardly immune to ominous cultural trends. With its particularisms and enduring piety towards a tragic past, the South, not surprisingly, is a special target for multiculturalists and other levellers of American traditions. The South that once celebrated Lee-Jackson Day and Confederate Memorial Day has long vanished; now attacks on simply flying the Confederate Battle Flag or playing the song "Dixie"—to name just two examples—are common and in many cases successful.

Beyond that, the achievements of Southern civilization are either ignored or ridiculed at all levels of American education. This chapter has discussed John Randolph of Roanoke and the Vanderbilt Agrarians. Today, Randolph is unknown to most students of American political history. Poetry by Ransom, Tate, and Warren may still make it to whatever new reading lists the textbook industry is currently churning out, but the Agrarians' substantial achievements in criticism and the creative arts are vastly underrepresented in academia. The Southern elite, whether political leaders, academics, the business class, or the media has mostly displayed timidity in the face of these assaults (in some cases, these gentlemen and/or institutions are leading the charge). As the Marxist historian and Southern sympathizer Eugene Genovese recently observed:

> We are witnessing a cultural and political atrocity—an increasingly successful campaign by the media and an academic elite to strip young white southerners, and arguably black southerners as well, of their heritage, and, therefore, their identity. They are being taught to forget their forebears or to remember them with shame. . . . Still, we may doubt that many young southerners believe that Jefferson Davis, Alexander Stephens, John C. Calhoun and James Henley Thornwell, Robert E. Lee and Stonewall Jackson were other than admirable men. It is one thing to silence people, another to convince them.[25]

And so, the bitter prophecies of Weaver and the Agrarians—namely, that a traditional society could not survive the social upheaval of industrialism, rampant capitalism or the dictates of a far-off, centralized state—are now being played out. Two world views are in conflict, with the result still uncertain. In a 1952 speech at a family reunion, Weaver acknowledged that traditionalists are engaged "in a battle against the dehumanization of life" that "has been a losing one for more than a hundred years." And yet, he maintained the South would remain a holdout, a bulwark against modernity. "We are provincials," he told his relatives. "We have our names on the land. These are great assets."[26]

A guide in this ongoing struggle is Weaver's vision of the South. Its political tradition was dedicated to the survival of a regional culture where a man can find happiness and contentment. If our enemy is the overbearing state, then our satisfaction comes from the more spiritual, nonmaterialistic things. From his study of Southern literature, Weaver discovered a vision of man's dual nature that is honest and enduring. Whether the Southern tradition at this late date can provide wisdom to a troubled nation is very much an open question. Even the wise counsel of Weaver or Lytle is not as assuring as it might have been decades ago. At the least, Weaver's work today can be read as a passionate plea for his fellow Southerners, even in their Sunbelt phase, to reflect on their heritage and remember who they are.

7

Barbarians in the Saddle: *Visions of Order*

Visions of Order completes the Weaver canon. He began writing the manuscript about two years after completing *The Ethics of Rhetoric*. Weaver received a $4,500 grant from the Volker Fund which allowed him to take a leave of absence from Chicago and finish the first draft. Revisions continued up until the early 1960s. After it was rejected by both Regnery Gateway and Farrar, Straus and Cudahy, Louisiana State University Press finally accepted the manuscript. However, the final decision was not made until March, 1963, only weeks before Weaver died of a heart attack in his Chicago hotel room.[1]

Visions of Order should be read as the successor to *Ideas Have Consequences*. As we have seen, Weaver was confident the Southern tradition would survive these current dark ages. But with *Visions of Order*, we again leave the world of a nonmaterialistic South for a modern world which has completely lost all its discriminating power to choose between good and evil. There are visions of order on these pages, but just as striking is a vision of society out of kilter and a portrait of modern man who has lost control of his destiny. The vision of a civilization in crisis is even more devastating than what appeared in *Ideas Have Consequences*. This should not be surprising. Like all great writers, Richard Weaver, from book to book and essay to essay, showed progress in both his writing skills and the development of ideas.

The increasingly apocalyptic vision is also due to the continued advances and even greater power technology held over our lives. Juggernaut technology had become a many-headed machine that inspired awe and admiration in modern man. But it was also a force that continued to destroy many of Weaver's cherished ideals. He acknowledged the downward spiral in the 1958 introduction to the paperback version of *Ideas Have Consequences*: "It seems to me that the world is now more than ever dominated by the gods of mass and speed and that the worship of these can lead only to the lowering of standards, the adulteration of quality, and, in general, to the loss of those things which are essential to the life of civility and culture. The tendency to look with suspicion upon excellence, both intellectual and moral, as 'undemocratic' shows no sign of diminishing."[2]

Familiar themes argued in previous books are addressed again in *Visions of Order*. These include education, the idea of progress, science, the need for distinctions and hierarchy, and the catastrophic consequences of total war. Some complaints were familiar, but new rounds of criticism are also attached to each subject.

On education, for instance, Weaver is influenced by Eric Voegelin's theory that the gnostism of the first and second century A.D. set Western thought on a downhill path to its current disastrous belief in the infallibility of man. Voegelin was fond of drawing the line from gnosticism to the triumph of totalitarianism in the twentieth century. For Weaver, gnosticism was a "subversive force" which saw man as a good, if not divine creature, and "in which the world at least partly represented evil." The consequences of gnosticism included an educational establishment that resents both the authority of the teacher and the entire "master/pupil" situation. In fact, the teacher can no longer be considered an authority figure because all authority is bad (again, Weaver's prophetic talents are on display; this is an "idea" that gained in circulation). Grades are bad because they may reveal some students have superior gifts and aptitudes than others. Such feelings of superiority are always bad—and undemocratic to boot. However, the student is a good, if not sainted, being because youth itself is always good and in the right. In short, the gnostic influence represented "a conflict between [educators] and the principle teachings of the Judeo-Christian heritage."[3]

"Childhood wisdom," Weaver noticed, was the rage among statist educators such as John Dewey. The focus is to "teach students, not knowledge." And what we must teach young people is to adapt to a "changing world," without ever asking why the world is changing (so we may then ask if such changes are good or not). Producing social democrats was the goal of public education in twentieth-century America and those teachers who dare question this may be fired for their dangerous dissent. Weaver recalls this was the exact fate a teaching colleague faced.

Earlier, Weaver took the public to task for expecting too much from public education. But now, he predicted Americans would reject these attempts at social indoctrination. He thought the challenge presented by the launching of the Russian satellite (the famous Sputnik shocker) would turn the tide back towards excellence and achievement. Weaver seemed hopeful Americans would eventually dismisss the "revolutionaries" running our public schools.

Had he lived, Weaver might have adjusted his thinking. Public opinion polls show Americans want to continue spending enormous amounts of money on their public schools. In addition, they generally rate the schools their own children attend as acceptable. As far as grades being bad, well, Weaver did not live to see a phenomenon that began in the early 1970s where several famous universities—Stanford and Brown among them—did away with failing grades altogether! Think about it. Young people swagger into well-known liberal arts universities, knowing full well that as long as they don't break any laws (indeed, if there are any laws that can be broken), he or she will never have to worry about receiving an "F" and thus no credit for any course they take. Students, I believe, either received A's or B's—and nothing lower. Recently, one of those famous universities adjusted their experiment somewhat by adding a "NP" ("no passing") grade to their rather undaunting standards.

The modern world's contempt for the past is illustrated with an even greater intensity in *Visions of Order*. The cult of "presentism" celebrates the twentieth century as superior to all past epochs. This, of course, has been a theme throughout Weaver's work. What is new here is his critique of the idolization of youth. Weaver notices his fellow Americans spending large sums of money on chemicals and surgery that promise to wipe out the aging process—the face stays young, the hair doesn't gray, the entire body is improved upon—in all, a vain effort to defeat the inevitablity of old age and mortality. With a dashing young couple in the White House, idolization of youth was in full swing during the early 1960s and continued with an even greater momentum throughout the decade. An unpopular war, a revolt against middle-class conformity, and the sexual revolution all romanticized youth as representing the most advanced stage of intelligence one might reach. Weaver would have sympathized for a revolt against materialism, but he surely would have been appalled to see it carried out by a New Left which like its predecessors, worshiped the Leviathan state.

Ideas Have Consequences captured the chaos of urban culture and the triumph of the masses that developed after World War II. *The Ethics of Rhetoric* was, in part, a commentary on a sterile society made by advances in science and technology and also on a nation that had succumbed to state worship. *Visions of Order,* similarly captures the mood of the early 1960s. Idolization of youth, the increased mobility of the general public, and as Americans became more prosperous, the "machine worship" of the new technology all continue the riveting commentary on a Western world wallowing in decadence. The generation that came of age in the 1960s, for instance, was hailed as the most idealistic, intelligent, and activist such group in American history. At least they were considered a darn sight better than the "silent generation" of the 1950s.

Weaver would certainly disagree with the idea that the sixties kids represented a new age of advanced wisdom. Nor would he defend the youth of the fifties as necessarily a superior generation to their successors. In either case, Weaver would simply offer that youth provides a vitality which is good for society, but that it is in no position for leadership or authority. Youth lacks experience, the wisdom gained from experience, and the ability to interpret events that such wisdom allows for. Idolization of youth is yet another ill-fated attempt to deny hard lessons of history and man's limitations. When Weaver ridiculed the idea of "wisdom and youth" he possibly had his own undergraduate fling with socialism in mind. It must have equally appalled and amused him that his energies directed towards a defense of traditionalism were once spent promoting socialism.

Our old friend King Science also makes an appearance in *Visions of Order.* Science, as expected by our society, offers modern man an enticing (and false) view of life: it will provide a prosperity so great as to change human nature. The physical feeding of man will be satisfied and he will live in peace with his neighbor. That we know from Weaver's earlier works. The thesis advanced in *Visions of Order* declares that science's great discoveries of the universe have denigrated the importance of man. The universe is large and infinite. Thus, in the scheme of things, man is a small and insignificant creature. His individual trials now matter very little. Tragedies in Greek and Elizabethan literature were important because they signified that man's existence, his decisions and his actions were monumental. But because it orders our lives for us, science has made tragedy impossible. And as Weaver ruefully noted in the book's last chapter, the disappearance of tragedy contributed greatly to the demise of great literature in the Western world.

Machine Worship

The two most compelling visions of a world spinning out of control come in chapters on total war and machine worship. Throughout his career, Weaver took up his pen against juggernaut technology. He could not stop the advance of science and technology, but he could examine the terrible consequences of its victories. In *Visions of Order* that means the invention of atomic weapons, airplanes, and automobiles. All these gadgets are *de rigueur* to us; no one can imagine life without the automobile, nearly all of us have traveled by airplane, and we have all lived in a world that possesses tens of thousands of nuclear weapons.

Still, Weaver wrote during the hot years of the Cold War when both American and Soviet officials talked openly of using nuclear weapons and incidents such as the Berlin Blockade and the Cuban Missile crisis seemed to push the world to the brink of destruction. Succeeding generations have learned to live with the bomb, but what is significant to Weaver is the acceptance of "total warfare." This dreadful phenomenon has stretched from the Civil War to World Wars I and II to finally, wars of genocide in Asia, Africa, and Europe.

On this subject, Weaver was characteristically candid. Those who wished to abolish war forever are "stabbing the wind." War itself is the logical conclusion when a people or nation feel they have been mortally wronged by other peoples or nations. Wars cannot be abolished, but the example of chivalry—when no man is ever outside the pale of brotherhood—can "humanize" war or at least make sure it is fought within certain guidelines: War is only made on armed men, it leaves women and children alone, and the loser is eventually brought back into the brotherhood of men. Total war ended all that. This is warfare practiced without discrimination among human beings. Women, children, elderly citizens, unarmed men—all were suddenly treated the same as soldiers in combat gear.

What does it all mean? The fall of the gentlemanly ideal was one calamity that led to total war. The gentleman—Weaver's examples are once again Washington and Lee, but also the fallen Union General George McClellan—would never have tolerated total war, but with distinctions of age, sex, class, education, and occupation all lost, every human being is fair game for mass destruction. Total warfare abroad deeply affects our own culture at home. First of all, there was a loss of innocence among a nation's youth and the end to the restraining powers which characterize the idea of civilization itself.

> These obliteration bombings carried on by both sides in the Second World War put an end to all discriminations. Neither status nor location offered any immunity from destruction, and that often of a horrible kind. Mass killing did in fact rob the cradle and the grave. Our nation was treated to the spectacle of young boys fresh out of Kansas and Texas turning nonmilitary Dresden into a holocaust which is said to have taken tens of thousands of lives. . . . These are items of the evidence that the war of unlimited objectives has swallowed up all discrimination, comparison, humanity, and, we would have to add, enlightened self-interest. Such things are so inimical to the foundations on which civilization is built that they cast into doubt the very possibility of recovery.[4]

Advances in "high-tech" weapons left man overwhelmed by his own gaudy inventions. Western man had become flattered by his own ingenuity. But he was not content to stop there. He found even more pleasure in his ability to use them. In an age of mass destruction, not even remnants of the old nobility were spared:

> It is more disturbing to think that the restraints which had been formed through religion and humanitarian liberalism proved too weak to stay the tide anywhere. We are compelled to recall Winston Churchill, a descendant of the Duke of Marlborough and in many ways a fit spokesman for Britain's nobility, saying that no extreme of violence would be considered too great for victory. Then there is the equally dismaying spectacle of Franklin D. Roosevelt, the reputedly great liberal and humanitarian, smiling blandly and waving the cigarette holder while his agents showered unimaginable destruction upon European and Japanese civilians.[5]

Weaver was not only blaming the allies, who, after all, were fighting global fascism. Both sides practiced total warfare. Indeed, Nazi Germany was the first nation to both develop intercontinental missiles, and during the Spanish Civil War, bomb civilians from the sky. One wants to step back and wonder why Weaver didn't direct more of his ire against the other side. What about Pearl Harbor? Wasn't that an example of total warfare? Or wasn't the Bataan Death March particularly barbaric in its treatment of wartime prisoners?

But Weaver's concern was the effect of total warfare on the souls of nations conceived in liberty and that still pledged fidelity to individual freedom and Judeo-Christian traditions. Total war, like the science which helped create it, terribly debased the spiritual nature of man. According to Weaver, the question was no longer: should man bomb an open city? Instead it was: if we can bomb an open city, then we *should* bomb an open city. This parallels a saying that arises throughout Weaver's later writings: if man is a beast, then by all means we must go ahead and let him behave like one.

Total war was also a consequence of machine worship. The latter itself was a baneful example of the forms or objects which define a civilization being given "an illicit status." Legal punishment in ancient Byzantium and eighteenth-century Europe and the Inquisitions of the Middle Ages were Weaver's examples of a society practicing a cruelty that belied their contributions to civilization. As with science and the centralized state, men were worshipping false gods.

> So it is that when a culture falls to the worshipping of the forms it has created, it grows blind to the source of cultural expression itself and may engender perverse cruelty. The degeneration may take the form of static arts, of barbarous legal codes in defense of conventions, or the inhuman sacrifice exacted by a brilliant technology. At some point, its delight in these things has clouded over the right ethical and other determinations of life.[6]

Are we in the West victims of excessive form worship? None would dare challenge the assumption that because we are part of the "developed" (i.e., industrialized) world, we are miles ahead of our sorry counterparts in the "underdeveloped" (i.e., agrarian) world. But as Weaver tersely points out, the developed West has carried form worship to an extreme. The Agrarians of course railed against industrialism, but here again is an example of the student surpassing his masters. The Agrarians, not even Lytle, made such a concentrated, riveting offensive against modernism as Weaver did in both the cases of total warfare and machine worship. Who wants to say anything bad about the automobile or airplane? They represent forms that flatter us in proving our superiority to all previous epochs. The "sleek body" of the airplane or automobile is "pleasing to the aesthetic sense." They provide a comfort and convenience we cannot live without. But they also provide a luxury so necessary to our lives that it justifies the tens of thousands of deaths they are responsible for in each passing year.

> The most appalling human sacrifice of Western society today is the toll taken by machine culture. As just suggested, our familiarity with these losses has caused us to accept them and to deaden our response to the horror of them. But suppose we make an attempt to see the facts with fresh eyes. In 1960 in this country alone about 38,000 lives were taken by automobile accidents. But we cannot stop with this figure. There occurred along with these deaths tens of thousands of injuries, some of them permanently disabling. The same things goes on in all of the modern Western countries. . . . To such figures there must be added the numbers taken by airplane accidents. I do not have statistics for civilian losses, but a statement given out not long ago by the United States Army Air Force shows that in peace time the annual number of fatalities from air accidents is about 550 young men—these being of course, among the physically finest of the race.[7]

Weaver assailed the anxiety the airplane brought to modern life. In a comparison Weaver would have appreciated, Troy Cauley, a contributor to *Who Owns America?*, the 1935 sequel to *I'll Take My Stand,* compares the emptiness of a cross-country airplane ride he had recently taken to his boyhood journeys to the farmer's market.

> When I was a small boy in central Texas we lived about nine miles from the county seat. . . . In the fall we took a bale of cotton to town in a wagon. With a load of this sort, the team of horses walked about four miles an hour along the dirt road, thus taking a little over two hours for the trip. A short time ago I flew from Texas to California in a 747 jet in about the same length of time. That looks like incredible progress. Let's examine it more closely. On the flight to California I saw virtually nothing of the country. From an elevation of 36,000 feet, all we saw were some weather-beaten clouds. Our seats were narrow and jammed together, but I visited with no one. Nobody showed any interest in me. I was in a crowd but it was a very lonely crowd. On the trip to town with the bale of cotton we visited with fellow-travellers along the way. We exchanged hearty greetings with neighbors as they sat on their porches. My brother and I had the whole back-end of the wagon in which to roll, tumble, and wrestle. We saw field-larks in the pastures and heard their cheerful calls. Bob-white quail thundered out of the bushes along the fence-rows. Jack-rabbits raced off for cover of the post-oaks. The trip was a big success even before we got to town.[8]

Weaver himself had no use for this invention which made the world smaller, thus forcing us into a much unwanted and anxiety-filled "global village." He once told Henry Regnery that a man has to "draw the line somewhere" and in Weaver's case it was the use of airplanes. Weaver only flew once in his life. Meeting a speaking engagement in

California, he enjoyed the scenery over the Grand Canyon, but preferred to take future journeys by railroad.[9]

The same was true for automobiles. With money won from the Quantrell Prize, Weaver bought an automobile but after experiencing great difficulty in navigating the back streets of Chicago's South Side, he thankfully gave up the machine.[10] Airplane deaths and automobile deaths eventually add up to nearly the same numbers as those caused by the terrible sword of total warfare. They are both galling examples of societies (and not just Western societies alone) that have succumbed to false gods:

> The air is filled with suggestion that modern Western culture represents a great humanitarian gain over any culture which has preceded it. Yet it would be very easy for some future people to regard ours as one of the most brutal cultures that ever existed. The statistics would be at hand to prove it as well as the stories and the photographs.[11]

Weaver's blistering criticism of machine worship continues to underscore his preference for a society in a pastoral setting. Granted, that is not going to happen anytime soon. Someday, the urban/industrial order will fall and traditional societies may return, but until then, man must somehow remain a reverent, pious being. Or as T.S. Eliot famously put it, he must "redeem the time." We cannot throw the past away. When that happens, then comes the utopian attempts to create a "new man" which in turn, can only lead to state control.

Piety takes many forms, but for Weaver a key element was retaining a sense of place. Even this virtue was threatened by a machine worship which has greatly abetted our love of mobility. In the immediate postwar years, Americans continued to be a people on the move. The flight from the countryside to the city was followed up by the flight from the city to newly built suburbs. Artificial towns were thrown up on thousands of acres of previously unspoiled countryside to accommodate middle-class Americans made mobile by both the automobile and New Deal prosperity (and later, fleeing the barbarism of urban America).

However, our modern-day mobility represented yet another wrecking of tradition. Mobility, Weaver declared, has destroyed our sense of place, thus our sense of piety. As an example consider how a pious man might view northern Virginia. Place is a foundation of regional cultures and when one invokes northern Virginia, a sense of place with all its history, tragedy, customs, traditions and mythology comes directly to mind. As the state which gave the young nation most of its first revolutionary leaders and presidents, northern Virginia occupies a majestic place in American history. There is also the tragic grandeur of Civil War battlefields. The marriage of blood and land gave birth to, as Andrew Lytle termed it, a republic of families. This in turn created recognizable cultures which served as a firm firewall of resistance to the schemes of the centralized state. Because it represents an established culture, northern Virginia offers, as Weaver would term it, a sense of isolation, privacy, continuity, and protection to those who share its heritage.

Americans of the 1950s and 1960s (and certainly today) were a mobile people. We continue to be a people that worships the idea of material progress. As a people constantly on the go, the sense of place is lost and the mythologies that define it have vanished as well. Without surviving mythologies, there is no longer a lasting history. What our grandparents did is no longer real to us. Without a surviving history, it follows that Civil War battlefields in northern Virginia can be destroyed in the name of the glittering promise of material riches. This example was inspired by recent headlines, the proposed building of a huge American history "theme park" just miles from the Manassas battlefield in northern Virginia. I use northern Virginia as an example because it does inspire a deeply felt sense of history. But modern northern Virginia is seeing its history destroyed by machine worship and the secular religion of infinite progress. A number of prominent American historians have joined the battle to save the northern Virginia countryside. Weaver, too, would see the controversy over the "theme park" as an example of how we lose our history when we destroy our sense of place.[12]

As with *The Ethics of Rhetoric*, *Visions of Order* did not receive a very large response. R.C. Woodward called the book a decent continuation of themes advanced in other Weaver volumes, but he also claimed *Visions* would be tough going for the general reader. While writing that the book contained "valuable essays" on "the decline of the West," Jeffrey Hart nonetheless called the prose in *Visions* "lifeless and academic." Hart, an admirer of *The Southern Tradition at Bay*, also criticized Weaver for not being "combative enough" with liberal foes who remain "politely nameless."[13]

Willmoore Kendall, however, was most enthusiastic in champion-

the book. Writing two years after Weaver's death, he lifted *Visons of Order* into elevated company, proclaiming it the successor to *The Federalist*. Kendall urged conservatives to "go read—nay, go *live with*—the book, until you have made its contents your own. It will prepare you, as no other book, not *even The Federalist* will prepare you for your future encounters with the protagonists of the Liberal Revolution, above all by teaching you how to drive the debate to a deeper level than that on which our present spokesmen are engaging the Liberals."[14]

Kendall praised the book for championing the idea of a hierarchy and for teaching "the correctness of the Christian picture of man." Mostly, Kendall cited Weaver's traditionalism: A hierarchy would "keep alive within itself, and develop in the people, 'historical memory,' i.e., knowledge of their own tradition—lest, in ignorance of them, they forget, like madmen, what and who they are."[15]

Much of Kendall's essay was ill-tempered, blasting Clinton Rossitor's interpretation of Weaver in the former's famous book on American conservatism, *The Thankless Persuasion*; slamming Russell Kirk's introduction to *Visions of Order* and, in general, claiming that most critics of Weaver were ignoramuses who didn't know what they were talking about. But his main thesis is compelling. *Visions of Order* filled in the "missing section" of *The Federalist*, by answering the question that that famous volume posed, but never answered: namely, how "we the people" should order our lives to become and remain virtuous citizens of a free Republic. Christendom, tradition, a responsible hierarchy. Although a man of the populist-leaning Southwest, Kendall apparently now understood the redeeming virtues of the Old South's aristocracy of achievement. For Kendall, *Visions of Order* represented the high water mark for the traditionalist wing of modern American conservatism.[16]

The pattern of assailing present trends and offering ways of recovery is also present in *Visions of Order*. There is little here about private property; the importance of piety—in this case memory is defended as "learning essential to the soul." Culture is once again defined as exclusive and inward looking. Weaver also champions a fluid society that combines status and function. Things "are and are becoming," he proclaims. Man alive is in a state of "being and doing." This is basically an explanation of what Southern liberals attempted to do after the Civil War. As we recall from *The Southern Tradition at*

Bay, the Old South aristocracy had by then reached a stage of petrification. They no longer had the imagination to lead the region. So liberals responded with a public school system that championed piety and sought to preserve a tradition which included political genius, military valor, the older religiousness, and an independent spirit. As the South moved into the twentieth century, it would still keep the virtues of its illustrious past alive. Or so the "first liberals" hoped.

But the most stirring defense of tradition in *Visions of Order*, I think, comes from Weaver's defense of the West's Judeo-Christian tradition. First, there is Weaver's defense of Jewish orthodoxy. Judaism, to Weaver, was a strong religion in the same way that the U.S. Constitution was a worthy document: it was a series of "thou shalt nots" that served as a bulwark against temptation. Orthodox Jews understood the great temptations posed by forms of artificial beauty. "They have expressed in their commandments against various things a rooted feeling that beauty may seduce us to step outside 'the way,'" an approving Weaver remarked. To counter temptations, Orthodox Jews have tended towards a somberness in dress and appearance (i.e., long beards, plain black and white clothing, women without excessive makeup, no attempts to hide the aging process) that seemed unnecessary, but ultimately works as an "extreme protest, even . . . an over-protection against things many people have yielded to."[17]

In his review, Kendall also writes of "the respective roles in a healthy culture of dialectic and rhetoric . . . " as one of the strong points in *Visions of Order*. Indeed, this was a partnership Weaver was constantly looking for in the ideal rhetor. Dialectic provides us with a proper definition of things. But rhetoric is needed to persuade and drive men to action. Weaver's example of such a partnership—the triumph of Christianity in a pagan world—provides for the most moving passages of the book. Here the partnership shines through. While Socrates could proclaim: "The one thing I know is that I know nothing," both the Jew and Christian, Weaver happily noted, could simply counter: The one thing I know is God. The Christian knew the story of Jesus and the fall of man. They knew man was prone to fall, but they also knew the glorious story of Jesus Christ and the love He held for each human being:

> Christianity provided all that Greek dialectic left out. It spoke to the feelings, and what seems of paramount significance, it had its inception in an historical fact. The

Christian always had the story of Jesus with which to start his homilies. He could argue from a fact, or at least what was accepted as one, and this at once put him on grounds to persuade. We may recall here Aristotle's observation that in conversing with the multitude you do not aim at fresh scientific instruction; you rest your arguments upon generally accepted principles and beliefs, or broadly speaking, on things received. Practically, the victory of Christianity over Hellenic rationalism bears out the soundness of this insight. The Christians have worked through the poetry of their great allegory and through appeal to many facts as having happened, for example, the lives of the saints.[18]

The Christian carried with them not only the existence of God, but a startling revelation taught by Jesus: Namely, that human life has meaning, and thus, each human being is important:

> The Greeks could out-argue the Christians and the Romans could subject them to their government, but there was in Christianity an ethical respect for the person which triumphed over these formalizations. Neither the beauty of Greek culture nor the grandeur of the Roman state system was the complete answer to what people wanted in their lives as a whole.[19]

Armed with this revolutionary idea, Christianity became the force that through the combination of dialectic and a persuasive rhetoric was able to withstand decades of persecution by the Romans, eventually outlasting that once-mighty empire.

> The triumph and continuance of Christianity and Christian culture attest the power of rhetoric in holding men together and maintaining institutions. It is generally admitted that there is a strong element of Platonism in Christianity. But if Plato provided the reasoning, Paul and Augustine supplied the persuasion. What emerged from this could not be withstood even by the power of Rome.[20]

Visions of Order is mostly a bleak book. In *Ideas Have Consequences*, Weaver railed against modern man as a spoiled child unable to reject demagogic leaders. That charge is somewhat modified here. Weaver, instead, sees man as a victim of overwhelming forces—total war, machine worship, the public education cabal dominated by progressives. The world of the hard-working yeoman farmer or the somber, responsible aristocrat is never far from Weaver's mind. That world, as Weaver again acknowledges has long been destroyed by the endless physical feeding of man who submits to becoming an economic unit.

Visions of Order thus provides another arresting vision of barbarism in the saddle. And yet, the triumph of Christianity over the Roman

Empire offers us a more pleasing example of man's ever-resilient spirit. In "Up From Liberalism," Weaver acknowledged the need for renewing the idea of a Christian society in a world that had just slaughtered tens of millions in its second world war of the century. Passages in *Vision of Order* continue to celebrate the Christian view of man and society. This most persistent critic of our world built by science and technology was equally a believer in the wonders of the human spirit. And the triumph of Christianity is a good enough example of the vision that inspired Weaver's hope for mankind.

8

Conclusion

The year after Weaver's death, Barry Goldwater won the Republican nomination for the presidency, thus representing a real and unexpected political victory for modern conservatism. Goldwater's nomination was strongly supported by the intellectual Right. Russell Kirk prepared speeches for Goldwater; Milton Freidman, Weaver's colleague at the University of Chicago, was an economic advisor and *National Review* publisher William Rusher was a chief organizer of a "draft Goldwater" campaign that had helped convince the reluctant senator he could win the Republican presidential nomination. But Goldwater's victory also touched off a wild media frenzy. The Arizonian was blasted as, among other things, an extremist, a warmonger, and a racist. In short, he was savaged by many of the ultimate "devil" terms Weaver described in *The Ethics of Rhetoric*. As quickly as conservative fortunes soared with Goldwater's nomination, they were just as rapidly deflated when Goldwater suffered a landslide defeat to President Lyndon Johnson.[1]

Goldwater's defeat dramatically affected the way conservatives viewed politics. While Goldwater was both a strong critic of such New Deal sacred cows as Social Security and the Tennessee Valley Authority and a states' rights advocate on explosive social issues, post-1964 conservatives tended to moderate their orthodoxy. In 1968, many Goldwaterites supported Richard Nixon over the far more conservative Ronald Reagan. Goldwater's defeat taught most conservatives to live with the New Deal (and LBJ's Great Society) and to surrender decentralizing doctrines championed by such earlier heroes as John Randolph and John C.

Calhoun. Ironically, Goldwater himself was part of this sea change. During the final years of his senatorial career, he denounced the "religious right" which flourished in the 1980s and more than once, found himself in opposition to such Old Right solons as North Carolina's Jesse Helms during heated debates on abortion and school prayer. Paul Gottfried and Thomas Fleming, writing in *The Conservative Movement*, summed up the consequences of 1964:

> The Goldwater campaign hurt the older conservatism in two ways; by equating social philosophy almost entirely with free enterprise; and contributing to a conservative movement more concerned with electoral victories than unifying principles. The multitude of activists, once assembled, became the major force among conservatives. A movement that [Russell] Kirk, citing T.S. Eliot, hoped would fight for the "permanent things" became increasingly concerned with opinion polls and electoral majorities.[2]

Into the void stepped a new movement, a feisty band of "neoconservative" intellectuals. Neoconservatives (Norman Podhoretz once remarked that "neoliberal" would have been a more accurate definition), were generally academics, mostly based in New York City. In addition, the neoconservative Right traced their lineage back to FDR's New Deal. While they opposed the excesses of the Great Society, neoconservatives could not bring themselves even to criticize the programs or the spirit of the New Deal. More than that, conservatives in general began viewing American civilization almost strictly as an "idea." "Ideas" such as democracy, capitalism (neatly combined into the "democratic capitalism" package), equality of opportunity, and an undefined diversity now defined the American experience.

Weaver disciples, especially M.E. Bradford, thought differently. Rather than such abstractions, Bradford, in his landmark studies on the U.S. Constitution and the Declaration of Independence, defined America in its laws, customs and codes of conduct as mostly an extension of the Anglo-Saxon world. (Bradford also noted that the Romans of the Old Republic had great influence on the Founding Fathers.) In short, the Founding Fathers were not "universalists," but products of a civilization with roots in Athens, Rome, Jerusalem, and London. The fragility of man and the institutions he creates were never far from their minds. America was not a "new Zion" but a neatly defined constitutional republic. None of this amounts to "multiculturalism."[3] Fleming and Gottfried starkly illustrated the dramatically different world views held by these competing strains of conservative thought:

[Traditionalists] live almost everywhere but New York, while neoconservatives are at home almost nowhere else. From the perspective of the [neoconservative] urban northeast, America is a society of immigrants held together by an ideology of democratic capitalism, but from the perspective of the [Old Right] South and nonurban Midwest, one is most impressed by the historical saga of flesh-and-blood men and women building, generation by generation, a community on the frontier. The Constitution, the Bill of Rights, and democratic capitalism would be viewed merely as artifacts of the American experience: they were made by Americans; they did not make America.[4]

Meanwhile, paleoconservatives failed poorly in important political struggles. After Ronald Reagan's presidential triumph in 1980, Washington and Manhattan conservatives pulled rank to defeat Bradford's bid to become head of the National Endowment for the Humanities. Bradford, like Goldwater in 1964, was victim of a media blitz, this one led by Heritage Foundation president Edwin Feulner and neoconservative guru Irving Kristol. Bradford's scholarly critique of the Lincoln legacy left him open to attacks as both a dangerous "neo-Confederate" sympathizer and an out-and-out racist. As one leading conservative boasted: "the Reagan Administration no more needs to sign on to Stephen Douglas Democrats than it does Tip O'Neill Democrats."[5]

During the Reagan era, there emerged a new conservative establishment, one dominated by Washington-based "think tanks" and neoconservative academics. This ascendant conservative establishment of the 1980s and 1990s, with its emphasis on unlimited economic growth and neverending free markets, saw no use for the Old Right or the antimodernist philosophy of Kirk and Weaver. But with the end of the Cold War, intramural conservative warfare broke out over numerous issues and events: the Persian Gulf War, trade, immigration, the George Bush-Patrick Buchanan presidential primary battle in 1992, and Buchanan's follow-up run in 1996. At times, the Old Right seemed close to tasting real victory: public opinion, for instance, swung heavily against both the nation's liberal immigration laws and "New World Order" foreign adventures in Haiti and Bosnia. In early 1996, Buchanan briefly had a real shot at gaining the GOP presidential nomination.

The paleoconservative heirs of Richard Weaver have not been defeated. In addition to public support, debates over post-Cold War military adventures, trade and immigration policies have revealed sympathy for Old Right positions from numerous Republican party members of Congress. Paleoconservatism carries on in journals such as

Chronicles, Modern Age, Southern Partisan, and at both the Rockford and Von Mises Institutes. Yet powerful forces in the Republican party and both the liberal and conservative East Coast media centers are solidly aligned against a resurgent Old Right. In addition to Bradford, other paleoconservative writers, namely Samuel Francis, Joseph Sobran, and Buchanan himself have seen their careers targeted for destruction by members of the Beltway Right. There is only so much "diversity of opinion" conservatives will tolerate. In short, the conservative wars of the 1990s have so far pitted the Old Right in a series of Pickett's Charges against the entrenched establishments in Washington and Manhattan.[6]

But the reigning conservative establishment has suffered its own share of defeats. When the cultural wars of the 1980s and 1990s took center stage, the Right was caught flat-footed. Multiculturalism, an ideology conservatives professed to despise, gained strong footholds not only in major universities, but also in fields of primary and secondary education. Multiculturalism came to define Western (and American) civilization as a reign of oppression, racism, and sexism, a way of life hardly worth saving. This is an evil dialectic, but even a false definition will fill a vacuum and eventually become the "truth." Conservatives, on the other hand, could only fall back on abstractions to define American civilization. "Democratic capitalism" became the Right's favorite god term. It hasn't worked. Such abstractions fail to conjure up the permanent things such as place and memory, blood and land, religion and mythology, concrete terms that Weaver, Kirk, and Bradford would all use in defining culture.

All in all, Weaver's influence has waned considerably in the decades following his death. Whether his antimaterialistic philosophy has any future in a society driven by rapid technological and social change seems a very troubled proposition. In the 1950s, despite enjoying critical and even popular success, Weaver strayed towards pessimism. Possibly because of the all-too-apparent triumph of a mass society in America and the prosecution of a second reconstruction in the South, Weaver seemed to grow more distant, perhaps more embittered. Friends noticed that the philosopher would sometimes go an entire year without seeing any close acquaintances. Weaver remained a bachelor, living and writing in a small Chicago hotel room, his books and essays retaining a loyal band of readers. However he felt about mid-twentieth-century America, Weaver knew the restoration of a moral society was possible, but only if a nation's citizens were willing to pay a steep price. At the end of *Ideas*, Weaver was hopeful for a revival of the "chivalry and spirituality of the Middle Ages," but he was also stern, asking hard questions of his fellow citizens:

> [We] have to inform the multitude that restoration comes at a price. Suppose we give them an intimation of the cost through a series of questions. Are you ready. . . . to grant that the law of reward is inflexible and that one cannot, by cunning or through complaints, obtain more than he puts in? Are you prepared to see that comfort may be a seduction and that the fetish of material prosperity will have to be pushed aside in favor of some sterner ideal? Do you see the necessity of accepting duties before you begin to talk of freedoms? These things will be very hard; they will call for deep reformation. It may well be that the course of degeneration has proved so enervating that there is no way of reinspiring with ideals.[7]

Richard Weaver should be read as one of the great post-World War II prophets of Western decline, especially of an alienated, rootless society. His vision, bleak as it seems, extends into many facets of modern life: High divorce rates, a declining standard of living, the dehumanizing aspects of a corporate economy, the destruction of civil communities, and the increasingly rancid assaults on America's founding Western heritage. When he wrote of modern men as "living like rats in the corner of broken cities," he presented a chilling portrait of life in the late 1940s; a view that has only intensified in succeeding decades.

This prophetic view has seemingly prevailed. On the brink of the twenty-first century, the triumph of science and technology looms larger than ever. We remain convinced the future belongs to science and science alone. The next few years will rumble with another round of hysterical optimism, all fueled by the strong belief that science will at last deliver us into an age of ease and comfort. Furthermore, man is still an economic unit, a consuming animal. The life of discipline and forging, of struggle and error, the grand drama where man's soul is at stake is deemed more and more irrelevant. Weaver, Davidson, Lytle, Bradford. Some days you get the feeling that the South's greatest export isn't cotton, tobacco, peaches or sugar, but producing prophets without honor in their own country.

Notes

Introduction: A Man Out of Step

1. See George Nash, *The Conservative Intellectual Movement in America* (New York: Basic Books, 1976): pp. 36–43 for a chapter highlighting Weaver's importance to the traditionalist wing of modern conservatism.

2. Weaver might agree with the description of the Old Republic as defined by Samuel Francis: "The essence of a republic, articulated by almost every theorist of republicanism from Cicero to Montesquieu, is the independence of the citizens who compose it and their commitment to a sustained active participation in its public affairs, the *res publica*. The very nature of the managerial revolution [of the early to mid-twentieth century] and the regime that developed from it promotes not independence, but dependency and not civic participation, but civic passivity." See Samuel Francis, *Beautiful Losers: Essays on the Failure of American Conservatism* (Columbia: University of Missouri Press, 1993): p. 17.

3. R. Emmett Tyrrell, Jr. *The Conservative Crackup* (New York: Simon and Schuster, 1992): p. 33. Tyrrell also takes Russell Kirk to task as a philosopher who also did not inspire political action among would-be conservatives. This is a highly dubious conclusion. Numerous conservative activists, not to mention many members of the U.S. Congress, received their introduction to intelligent conservative thought from reading *The Conservative Mind.*

4. Also linking the strategy of the Civil War to World War II is Murray Rothbard in "The Concepts of A 'Just War.'" *Southern Partisan* (Third Quarter, 1995): pp. 18–23. In typically pungent language, Rothbard declares: "By targeting and butchering civilians, Lincoln, Grant, and Sherman paved the way for all the genocidal horrors of the monstrous twentieth century." This view echoes Weaver's own conclusions in *Visions of Order.*

5. Allen Tate. *Essays of Four Decades* (Chicago: Swallow Publishers, 1968): p. 338.

1. Philosopher from Dixie

1. Conversation with Josephine Osborne, cousin of Richard M. Weaver. June, 1994.
2. Richard M. Weaver. "A Pattern Of Life." *Southern Partisan* (Fall, 1981): p. 13.
3. Kendall Beaton. "Richard M. Weaver: A Clear Voice in an Addled World." Unpublished essay, 1964. p. 1.
4. Richard M. Weaver. "Up From Liberalism," *Modern Age* (Winter 1958–59): p. 22.
5. Clifford Amyx. "Weaver The Liberal: A Memoir." *Modern Age* (Spring, 1987): pp. 103–4.
6. "Up From Liberalism," p. 23.
7. M.E. Bradford and George Core. Introduction to *The Southern Tradition at Bay* (Washington, D.C.: Regnery Gateway, 1989): p. 8. Conversation with Professor Ted J. Smith III, June, 1995.
8. Henry Regnery, "A Southern Agrarian at the University of Chicago," *Modern Age* (Spring, 1988): p. 112.
9. Wilma R. Ebbitt. "Richard M. Weaver, Teacher Of Rhetoric," *Georgia Review* (Winter, 1963): pp. 416–17.
10. Wilma R. Ebbitt. "Richard M. Weaver: Friend and Colleague." Unpublished essay, 1988, pp. 4–5. Edward Shils, "Liberalism: Collectivist and Conservative," *Chronicles* (July 1989): p. 12. Conservation with Polly Weaver Beaton, sister of Richard M. Weaver, August, 1993. Kendall Beaton, "Richard M. Weaver: A Clear Voice in an Addled World," p. 3. Fred Hobson, *Tell About the South: The Southern Rage to Explain* (Baton Rouge: Louisiana State University Press, 1983): p. 323. Walter Sullivan. "Richard Weaver and the Bishop's Widow." From *In Praise of Blood Sports and Other Essays.* (Baton Rouge: Louisiana State University Press, 1990): p. 37. Wilma R. Ebbitt. "Richard M. Weaver, Teacher of Rhetoric," p. 415.
11. Marion Montgomery, "Richard M. Weaver, 1948," *Modern Age* (Summer/Fall, 1982): p. 255. Fred Hobson, *Tell About the South*, p. 331. Russell Kirk, "Richard M. Weaver, R.I.P., *National Review* (April 23, 1963): p. 308. Also see Eugene Davidson, "Richard Malcolm Weaver—Conservative," *Modern Age* (Summer 1963): pp. 226–30. E. Victor Milione, "The Uniqueness of Richard M. Weaver," *Intercollegiate Review II* (September, 1965): p. 67. Frank S. Meyer, "Richard M. Weaver: An Appreciation," *Modern Age* (Summer/Fall, 1970): pp. 243–48.
12. Russell Kirk, *The Sword of Imagination: Memoirs of a Half-Century of Literary Conflict* (Grand Rapids: William B. Eerdmans Publishing Company, 1995): p. 175.

2. An Aristocracy of Achievement

1. Richard M. Weaver, *The Southern Tradition at Bay: A History of Postbellum Thought* (Washington, D.C.: Regnery Gateway, 1989): p. 43.
2. Calvin Brown, "Southern Nationalism and American Materialism." *The Southern Literary Quarterly,* vol. 1, no. 2 (Spring, 1969).
3. *The Southern Tradition at Bay*, p. 36.
4. For Weaver's acceptance of Christian discipline in the wake of World War II, see Richard M. Weaver, "Up From Liberalism," *Modern Age 2* (Winter, 1958–59): p. 21–32.

5. Allen Tate, "Remarks on the Southern Religion," from *I'll Take My Stand: The South and the Agrarian Tradition* (Baton Rouge: Louisiana State University Press, 1977): pp. 155–76.

6. W. J. Cash, *The Mind of The South* (New York: Vintage Books, 1941). A book that influenced the younger Weaver who was still in the clutches of socialism was John Crowe Ransom's *God Without Thunder: An Unorthodox Defense of Orthodoxy* (New York: Harcourt, Brace and Company, 1930).

7. *The Southern Tradition at Bay*, p. 95.

8. See Russell Kirk, *Randolph of Roanoke: A Study in American Politics* (Indianapolis: Liberty Press, 1978) for a biography of an early American statesmen whose motto "I am a gentleman. I love liberty, I hate equality" has served as a guiding principle for the modern-day conservatism founded by both Weaver and Kirk.

9. For laudatory views of Lee's post-Civil War life, see *Lee: The Last Years* by Charles Bracelen Flood (Boston: Houghton Mifflin Company, 1981) and *Personal Reminiscences of General Robert E. Lee* by Rev. J. William Jones, D.D. (Richmond: United States Historical Society Press, 1989). For a dissenting view, see Andrew Lytle, "Robert E. Lee." In *From Eden to Babylon: The Social and Political Essays of Andrew Nelson Lytle* (Washington: Regnery Gateway, 1989): pp. 97–108. Lytle dismisses the notion that "the training of a few thousand students" could make any difference when the terms of surrender had been broken and Radical Republicans carried out reconstructionist policy whose aims were "the destruction of Southern civilization."

10. M. E. Bradford, *A Better Guide Than Reason: Federalists and Anti-Federalists* (New Brunswick: Transaction Publishers, 1994): pp. 79–97.

11. *The Southern Tradition at Bay*, p. 42.

12. For a comparison of a virtuous Old South political leader (former Texas governor Coke Stevenson) to a more corruptible New South figure (former president Lyndon Johnson), see M.E. Bradford, "Poisoned at the Source" in *Against The Barbarians* (Columbia: University of Missouri Press, 1993): pp. 222–29. Here Bradford agrees with biographer Robert Caro that Johnson was something less than a principled modern-day liberal. While Stevenson was a low-keyed conservative Southern senator, Johnson, Bradford charges, was "never either liberal or a conservative, but . . . a man always hungry for power and interested in what might be done with it."

13. Thomas Landess. "Is the Battle Over . . . Or Has It Just Begun? The Southern Tradition Twenty Years After Richard M. Weaver." *Southern Partisan* (Spring, 1983): p. 17.

14. *The Southern Tradition at Bay*, p. 289.

15. Ibid., pp. 365, 366.

16. Ibid., p. 184.

17. Ibid., p. 213.

18. Richard M. Weaver, "The South and The American Union," from *The Southern Essays of Richard M. Weaver*, ed. by George Curtis III and James J. Thompson, Jr. (Indianapolis: Liberty Press): p. 256.

19. *The Southern Tradition at Bay*, p. 329. Also see Donald Davidson, *Southern Writers in the Modern World* (Athens, University of Georgia Press, 1958): p. 33. Davidson recalled that his father gave him the middle name Grady after the leading public champion of a New South. Davidson was not proud of being linked to "the admirable Peacemaker." He wrote: "I dutifully exulted in it [the name] until, through some uneasiness that I cannot explain, I discarded it in early college days and have since avoided it except for purposes of legal identification."

20. *The Southern Tradition at Bay*, p. 362, 363.
21. Ibid., p. 360.
22. Weaver might have have appreciated comments made in 1870 by Queen Victoria to Sir Theodore Martin: "The Queen is most anxious to enlist everyone to join in checking this mad, wicked folly of women's rights. Woman would become the most hateful, heartless and disgusting of human beings, were she allowed to unsex herself." From "Where Have All The Women Gone?" by Mark Racho, *Chronicles,* (May, 1995): pp. 26–28.
23. *The Southern Tradition at Bay*, p. 265.
24. Ibid., p. 289.
25. Comments by Ford Maddox Ford, gathered in "Conference on Literature and Reading, 1935," in *The Southern Review and Modern Literature,* (Baton Rouge: Louisiana State University Press, 1985): p. 77, carry the same theme: the distinctiveness of Southern culture, namely its literature, might show the world the way out of the grip of totalitarianism that raged throughout the 1930s. "And finally, you—the South—have the ball of the world at your feet. If you desire it, the most glorious of revenges is there for your taking. You were conquered in a war; now at peace, you are conquering the conqueror of your former conquerors. That is the *revanche noble!*'"
26. *The Southern Tradition at Bay*, p. 377.

3. Man in Megalopolis

1. Richard M. Weaver. "Up From Liberalism," *Modern Age 2* (Winter, 1958–59): pp. 21–32.
2. Conversation with Ted J. Smith III, June, 1995.
3. Richard M. Weaver, *Ideas Have Consequences* (Chicago: The University of Chicago Press, 1948): p. 3.
4. Ibid., p. 4.
5. Willmoore Kendall. "How To Read Richard Weaver: Philosopher of We the [Virtuous] People." *Intercollegiate Review II* (September, 1965): pp. 77–86.
6. *Ideas Have Consequences*, p. 85.
7. Ibid., p. 87.
8. See Andrew Lytle, "The Hind Tit." From *I'll Take My Stand: The South and The Agrarian Tradition* (Baton Rouge: Louisiana University Press, 1977): pp. 217–29. For Lytle, the sanctity of work was also preserved in an agrarian culture. Describing the female's task of churning butter, Lytle observed, "The process has been long, and to some extent, tedious, but profitable, because insomuch as it has taken time and care and intelligence, by that much does it have a meaning."
9. *Ideas Have Consequences,* p. 179.
10. Ibid., p. 43.
11. Ibid., pp. 114–15.
12. Richard M. Weaver, "The Meaning of Name and Place," *Southern Partisan* (Spring/ Summer, 1981): p. 15.
13. *Ideas Have Consequences,* pp. 63–64.
14. For a portrait of Weaver's life in Chicago by a friend and supporter, see Russell Kirk, *The Sword of Imagination: Memoirs of a Half-Century of Literary Conflict* (Grand Rapids: William B. Eerdmans Publishing Company, 1995): pp. 172–76.
15. *Ideas Have Consequences,* p. 136.

16. Donald Davidson, "The Mystery of The Agrarians," *Saturday Review* 26 (23 January 1943): p. 7.
17. W.A. Orton. Review of *Ideas Have Consequences. Commonweal* (May 14, 1948): p. 120.
18. George Geiger. "We Note . . . the Consequences Of Some Ideas." *Antioch Review* (June, 1948): pp. 251–54. Herbert I. Muller. "The Revival Of The Absolute." *Antioch Review* (March, 1949): pp. 99–110. W.E. Garrison. "Unraveling Mr. Weaver." *The Christian Century* (May 5, 1948): p. 416.
19. See the paperback edition of *Ideas Have Consequences* (Chicago: University of Chicago Press, 1959) for quotations by Ransom, Tillich, and Niebuhr. John Fermatt. Review of *Ideas Have Consequences. The Catholic World* (June, 1948): p. 278.
20. Willmoore Kendall. Review of *Ideas Have Consequences.* In *Journal of Politics* II (February, 1949): p. 261. Frank Meyer. "Richard M. Weaver: An Appreciation. *Modern Age* (Summer/Fall, 1970): pp. 243–48.
21. See William Kauffman, *America First!: Its History, Culture and Politics* (Amherst, NY: Prometheus Books, 1995): pp. 69–85 for a lively study of anti-New Deal American authors.
22. Chilton Williamson, Jr. "Richard Weaver: Stranger in Paradise." *National Review* (December, 31, 1985): pp. 96–98. To underline his point, Williamson scorns the utopian impluse of modern-day conservatism: "According to the new "conservative" . . . creeds, the sky is the clear, clear limit, with no cloud to be seen threatening diaster from resource depletion, environmental depredation, crowd culture, uncontrolled immigration from Third World countries, the dehumanizing effects of technology, or metaphysical materialism—-so long, of course, as all the proper prescriptions, as handed down by . . . 'conservative' think-tanks are conscientiously applied." "The Adverse Descent" title was learned by the author in a conversation with Professor Ted J. Smith III, June, 1995.

4. State Worship

1. Kendall Beaton, "Richard Weaver: A Clear Voice in an Addled World." Unpublished essay, p.1.
2. Richard M. Weaver, *The Ethics of Rhetoric* (Chicago: Regnery Gateway, 1953): p. 20.
3. Fred Hobson. "Richard Weaver." From *Tell about the South: The Southern Rage to Explain* (Baton Rouge: Louisiana State University Press, 1983): p. 326.
4. *The Ethics of Rhetoric*, pp. 169–70.
5. John Bliese, "Richard Weaver: Rhetoric and the Tyrannizing Image." *Modern Age* (Fall, 1988): p. 210.
6. *The Ethics of Rhetoric*, p. 168.
7. Frank Meyer. *The Conservative Mainstream* (New Rochelle: Arlington House, 1969): pp. 470–72.
8. It must be noted, however, that Lincoln was never a very popular president. He won elections by small margins in both 1860 and 1864. Because of those small mandates and his desire to go easy on the defeated South, there is reason to believe that the Radical Republicans would have moved to disable his presidency just as they similarly destroyed the administration of Andrew Johnson, Lincoln's ill-fated successor who opposed harsh Reconstruction-era measures taken against the South.

9. Russell Kirk, "Ethical Labor," *Sewanee Review* (July, 1954): pp. 490–91.
10. *The Ethics of Rhetoric*, p. 71.
11. Conversation with Louis Demelow, April, 1993. Mr. Demelow was one of Weaver's closest Chicago friends.
12. Richard M. Weaver. "The Middle of the Road: Where It Leads." *Human Events* (March 24, 1956): p. 8.
13. For two critiques of the Reaganite 1980s by disillusioned conservatives, see Samuel Francis, *Beautiful Losers: Essays on the Failure of American Conservatism* (Columbia: University of Missouri Press, 1993) and Larry Schwab, *The Illusion of a Conservative Reagan Revolution* (New Brunswick: Transaction Publishers, 1991).
14. *The Ethics of Rhetoric*, p. 183.
15. Ibid., p. 230.
16. For an excellent discussion of the Bryan—Darrow showdown, see Thomas Landess, "Is The Battle Over . . . Or Has It Just Begun: The Southern Tradition Twenty Years After Richard Weaver," *The Southern Partisan* (Spring, 1983): pp. 16, 17.
17. *The Ethics of Rhetoric*, p. 228.
18. Ibid., p. 220.
19. Ibid., p. 229.
20. "Ethical Labor," pp. 487, 503.
21. "Is The Battle Over . . . Or Has It Just Begun?" pp. 14, 17.

5. The Conservative's Sage

1. Richard M. Weaver. Unpublished essay, the "YAF acceptance speech," 7 March 1962. Courtesy of Josephine Osborne, cousin of Richard Weaver.
2. Richard M. Weaver, "The South and The American Union," from *The Southern Essays of Richard M. Weaver*, edited by George M. Curtis III and James H. Thompson, Jr. (Indianapolis: Liberty Press, 1987). pp. 230–56.
3. Richard M. Weaver, *Life Without Prejudice* (Chicago: Regnery Gateway, 1965): pp. 158–59.
4. Ibid., p. 21.
5. See Donald Davidson. *Regionalism and Nationalism in the United States: The Attack on Leviathan* (New Brunswick: Transaction, 1992) for the finest Agrarian statement on the importance of regional cultures.
6. Of course, Weaver was not some stuffy philistine who disliked the arts. In a healthy society, censorship is unnecessary. Healthy societies will produce artists who give us a fresh treatment of the human condition. Such societies flourish artistically because they have realized freedom from obscenity. They know the complexities of the human condition and will steer away from sentimentality. The creative arts in such a society will dwell on the tragedies and comedies of the human experience in a way that is both subtle and effective. According to Weaver, a healthy society doesn't need censorship because it has a vision of man and society that is "steady and whole."
7. Richard Weaver, *The Southern Tradition at Bay,* p. 379.
8. Weaver would have appreciated Wendell Berry's own definition of healthy regional cultures. "A culture capable of preserving land and people can be made only within a relatively stable and enduring relationship between a local people and its place. Community cultures made in this way would necessarily differ, and sometimes radically so, from one place to another, because places differ. This is

the true and necessary pluralism. There can, I think, be no national policy of pluralism or multiculturalism but only these pluralities of local cultures. And if these cultures are of any value and worthy of any respect, they will not be elective . . . but will be formed in response to local nature and local needs." See Wendell Berry, *Sex, Economy, Freedom & Community* (New York: Pantheon Books, 1993): p. 171.

6. The Nation's Stepchild

1. In a line that echoes Weaver's own hopes, Andrew Nelson Lytle once wrote, "Everywhere else in the nation's "progress" there has been a succession of triumphs, until now. I would hazard the guess, when the true crisis comes, as it will, that a Southern-born man will step forward and meet it. This because he has known defeat of his society, because he has eaten his bread in sorrow—in effect, because he knows what the world is, that it is not all teatty." See Andrew Nelson Lytle, "The Long View," from *Eden to Babylon: The Social and Political Essays of Andrew Nelson Lytle* (Washington: Regnery Gateway, 1989): pp. 187–88.
2. *The Southern Essays of Richard M. Weaver*, ed. George Curtis III and James J. Thompson, Jr. (Indianapolis: Liberty Press, 1987): pp. 230–31.
3. M.E. Bradford, "Not in Memoriam, But in Affirmation." From *Why the South Will Survive: Fifteen Southerners Look at their Region a Half Century After I'll Take My Stand*, edited by Clyde Wilson (Athens: University of Georgia Press, 1981): p. 252.
4. *The Southern Essays of Richard M. Weaver*, p. 188.
5. M.E. Bradford. "The Agrarianism of Richard Weaver: Beginnings and Completions." *Modern Age* (Summer-Fall, 1970): p. 252.
6. *The Southern Essays of Richard M. Weaver*, pp. 100–1.
7. Ibid., p. 100.
8. Ibid., p. 115.
9. On a *Firing Line* program hosted by William F. Buckley that took up the usual subject on why the South has a great literature, Walker Percy commented that the South's defeat in the Civil War played its part in the Southern Renaissance. Buckley countered that Japan and Germany lost World War II, but they didn't produce much of a literature afterwards. Percy, echoing Weaver in "The South And The American Union," noted that those two countries, unlike the defeated South, were beneficaries of the Marshall Plan and other economic rescue programs. See Jay Tolson, *Pilgrim in the Ruins: A Life of Walker Percy* (New York: Simon and Schuster, 1992): pp. 375–77. Allen Tate, *Essays of Four Decades* (Chicago: Allan Swallow Company, 1968): p. 592.
10. *The Southern Essays of Richard M. Weaver*, p. 227.
11. Cleanth Brooks, *William Faulkner: First Encounters* (New Haven: Yale University Press, 1983): p. 224. The entire book is an excellent introduction to Faulkner by the century's premier Faulkner scholar.
12. *The Southern Essays of Richard M. Weaver*, p. 70.
13. Thomas Wolfe, *Look Homeward, Angel: A Story of a Buried Life* (New York: Scribners, 1957): p. 465.
14. B. R. McElderry Jr. *Thomas Wolfe* (New York: Twayne Publishers, 1964): pp. 17–18.
15. *The Southern Essays of Richard M. Weaver*, p. 73.

16. Ibid., p. 8.
17. Ibid., p. 8.
18. Twelve Southerners, *I'll Take My Stand: The South and the Agrarian Tradition* (Baton Rouge: Louisiana State University Press, 1977): p. xliii.
19. *The Southern Essays of Richard M. Weaver*, p. 23.
20. Donald Davidson. "The Mystery of the Agrarians: Facts and Illusions About Some Southern Writers." *Saturday Review of Literature* (January 23, 1943): p. 6. Allen Tate to Donald Davidson in *The Literary Correspondence of Donald Davidson and Allen Tate,* edited by John Tyree Fain and Thomas Daniel Young, (Athens: University of Georgia Press, 1974): p. 328. Davidson, however, disagreed with Weaver that *I'll Take My Stand* received much of a positive reception in the North: "I'm not sure there was really more friendliness in the North than in the South," Davidson wrote Weaver on 25 March 1949. "The reviews were terrible. The Northern intellectuals were preparing to go Communist, and they hated us from the start. Our chief Northern advocates were probably to be found (we later discovered) among the Catholics, especially the Jesuits." Davidson to Weaver, 25 March 1949. The Davidson papers at the Jean and Alexander Heard Library's Special Collections, Vanderbilt University, Nashville, Tenn.
21. *The Southern Essays of Richard M. Weaver*, p. 12.
22. In the 1950s, Davidson wrote to his friend Russell Kirk, asserting that "living in Nashville and teaching at Vanderbilt University is very hard on a Southern Agrarian, I can assure you. It is, in fact, nothing but warfare, and we can't survive very long without some place to lick our wounds for a while." See Russell Kirk, introduction to *The Tennessee, The New River: Civil War to TVA*, vol. 2 by Donald Davidson (Nashville: J.S. Sanders & Company, 1992): p. xiii.
23. *The Southern Essays of Richard M. Weaver*, p. 28.
24. Responding to an interviewer's question on the subject, Andrew Lytle remarked: "We couldn't imagine it (the South's transformation from an agrarian to industrial culture) being as bad as it is now. You know, we were just protesting. The only thing that brought us into the public view was the Great Depression. And it (*I'll Take My Stand*) came out about that time, so we seemed prophets. At least, not prophets then, but they think we were prophets now. " See *Eden To Babylon: The Political and Social Essays of Andrew Nelson Lytle,* p. 251. Fred Hobson, *Tell about the South: The Southern Rage to Explain,* p. 353.
25. Eugene Genovese, *The Southern Tradition: The Achievement and Limitations of an American Conservatism* (Cambridge: Harvard University Press, 1994): p. xii.
26. Richard M. Weaver. "The Meaning of Name and Place," p. 16.

7. Barbarians in the Saddle

1. The preface by Ted J. Smith III in *Visions of Order*, by Richard M. Weaver (Bryn Mawr: Intercollegiate Studies Institute, 1995) contains a thorough publishing history of Weaver's last completed book.
2. *Ideas Have Consequences*, p.vi.
3. Eric Voeglin, *The World of the Polis* (Baton Rouge: Louisiana State University Press, 1957).
4. Richard M. Weaver, *Visions of Order: The Cultural Crisis of Our Time* (Bryn Mawr: Intercollegiate Studies Institute, 1995): pp. 98–99.
5. Ibid., p. 99.

6. Ibid., p. 87.
7. Ibid., p. 83.
8. Troy Cauley. "Who Own America?... Fifty Years Later." *Southern Partisan* (Winter, 1986): p. 32.
9. Henry Regnery. "A Southern Agrarian at the University of Chicago." *Modern Age* (Spring, 1988): p. 103.
10. Wilma Ebbitt. "Richard M. Weaver: Friend and Colleague." Unpublished essay, 1988, p. 4.
11. *Visions of Order*, p. 84.
12. In October, 1994, the Disney Corporation, bowing to heavy public criticism, decided against building the theme park in an area of Northern Virginia close to the Manassas Battlefield. The company said it would still look elsewhere in Virginia for prime real estate to build its park.
13. R.C. Woodward, review of *Visions of Order*, in *Library Journal* (July, 1964). Jeffrey Hart. Review of *Visions of Order* in *National Review* (30 June 1964).
14. Willmoore Kendall. "How To Read Richard Weaver, Philosopher of We the [Virtuous] People." *Intercollgiate Review II* (September, 1965): p. 86.
15. Ibid., p. 86.
16. Ibid., p. 85.
17. *Visions of Order*, p. 87.
18. Ibid., p. 66.
19. Ibid., p. 88.
20. *Visions of Order,* p. 67. For a further discussion of Weaver's Christian vision, see John P. East, "Richard M. Weaver" in *The American Conservative Movement: The Philosophical Founders* (Washington: Regnery Books, 1986): pp. 45–52.

8. Conclusion

1. See George Nash in *The Conservative Intellectual Movement in America* (New York: Basic Books, 1976) for conservative disillusionment with the media over the 1964 campaign. Attacks on Goldwater included those by Arkansas Senator William Fulbright: "Goldwater Republicanism is the closest thing in American politics to an equivalent of Russian Stalinism"; Martin Luther King, Jr.: "We see dangerous signs of Hitlerism in the Goldwater campaign"; and labor leader Walter Reuther: "Goldwater is mentally unbalanced—he needs a psychiatrist."
2. Paul Gottfried, *The Conservative Movement*, revised edition (New York: Twayne, 1993.): pp. 41–42.
3. See M.E. Bradford. *A Better Guide Than Reason: Federalist and Anti-Federalists* (New Brunswick: Transaction Publishers, 1994) for a study of the cultural roots of both the U.S. Constitution and the Declaration of Independence.
4. *The Conservative Movement*, p. 43.
5. Quoted in Samuel Francis. "The Legacy of M.E. Bradford." *Southern Partisan* (Fourth Quarter, 1992): p. 48. Conservatives who opposed Bradford discovered that, unfortunately, what goes around comes around. Several years after Bradford's "paper trail" deemed him unacceptable for the NEH post, conservative favorite Robert Bork was similarly savaged, this time by the Left, for his own scholarly writings, which liberals declared made Judge Bork unfit to sit on the Supreme Court. Henceforth, Republican administrations began looking for Supreme Court nominees who thankfully left behind no body of published work, scholarly or otherwise, that might be used against them.

6. Old Right opposition to the Persian Gulf War was a watershed event in the conservative wars of the 1990s. Both Sobran and Buchanan were against the war. Sobran's opposition cost him his job as senior editor at *National Review*. Since then, scores of newspapers have also dropped his syndicated column. However, attempts to have Buchanan's own column eliminated from hundreds of newspapers across the country failed. Francis, on the other hand, was fired from his editorial page position at the *Washington Times* in the summer of 1995 after being constantly monitored by a conservative foundation called the Center for Equal Opportunity. A young employee at the foundation declared, "I'm essentially running a one-man crusade to get this man [Francis] kicked out of the conservative movement." See "The Rise and Fall of a Paleoconservative at the *Washington Times*," part II by Samuel Francis, *Chronicles*, (May, 1996): pp. 43–45.
7. *Ideas Have Consequences,* pp. 186–87.

Bibliography

Books by Richard M. Weaver

Ideas Have Consequences. Chicago: The University of Chicago Press, 1948 (reprinted in paperback, 1950).

The Ethics of Rhetoric. Chicago: Henry Regnery Co. 1953 (reprinted in 1985 in the United States by Hermagoras Press, Davis, Calif.).

Composition: A Course in Reading and Writing. New York: Holt, Rinehart, and Winston, 1957 (revised with the assistance of Richard S. Beal and reprinted as *Rhetoric and Composition,* 2nd ed. 1967).

Visions of Order: The Cultural Crisis of Our Time. Baton Rouge: Louisiana State University Press, 1964 (reprinted in 1995 by Intercollegiate Studies Institute, Bryn Mawr, Penn.).

Life Without Prejudice and Other Essays. Chicago: Henry Regnery Co., 1965.

The Southern Tradition at Bay: A History of Postbellum Thought, edited by George Core and M.E. Bradford. New Rochelle, N.Y.: Arlington House, 1968 (reprinted in 1989 by Regnery Gateway, Washington, D.C.).

Language is Sermonic: Richard M. Weaver on the Nature of Rhetoric, edited by Richard L. Johannesen, Rennard Strickland, and Ralph T. Eubanks. Baton Rouge: Louisiana State University Press, 1970 (reprinted in paperback, 1985).

The Southern Essays of Richard M. Weaver, edited by George M. Curtis III and James J. Thompson, Jr. Indianapolis: Liberty Press, 1987.

Essays, Reviews, and Pamplets by Richard M. Weaver

"The Older Religiousness in the South," *Sewanee Review,* LI (April, 1943): pp. 237–49.

"Albert Taylor Bledsoe," *Sewanee Review,* LII (January, 1945): pp. 34–45.

"The South and the Revolt of Nihilism," *South Atlantic Quarterly,* XLIII (April, 1944): pp. 194–98.

"Southern Chivalry and Total War," *Sewanee Review*, LIII (April, 1945): pp. 267–78.
"Scholars or Gentlemen?" *College English*, VII (November, 1945–46): pp. 72–77.
Review of Leo Baeck, *The Pharisees and Other Essays, Commonweal,* XLVI, (1947): p. 484.
Review of Robert Rylee, *The Ring and the Cross, Commonweal,* XLVII (1947–48): pp. 46–48.
Review of Ward Moore, *Greener Than You Think, Commonweal,* XLVII (1947–48): pp. 179–80.
Review of Hermann Broch, *The Sleepwalkers, Commonweal,* XLVII (1947–48): pp. 620–22.
"The Etiology of the Image," *Poetry*, LXXII (June, 1948): pp. 156–61 (review of Rosemond Tuve, *Elizabethean and Metaphysical Imagery*).
"Orbis Americanum," *Sewanee Review*, LVI (1948): pp. 319–23 (review of Henry B. Parkes, *The American Experience* and Leo Gurko, *The Angry Decade*).
"Lee the Philosopher," *Georgia Review*, II (Fall, 1948): pp. 297–303.
"To Write the Truth," *College English*, X (October, 1948): pp. 25–30.
Review of Beatrice Webb, *Our Partnership, Commonweal,* XLVIII (1948): pp. 166–67.
Review of Charles A. Lindbergh, *Of Flight and Life, Commonweal,* XLVIII (1948): pp. 573.
Review of *The Diary of Pierce Loval, Commonweal,* XLIX (1948–49): pp. 122.
"Culture and Reconstruction," *Sewanee Review*, LVII (1949): pp. 714–18 (review of T.S. Eliot, *Notes Towards a Definition of Culture*).
"The Rhetoric of Social Science," *Journal of a General Education*, IV (1949–50): pp. 189–201.
Review of Samuel H. Beer, *The City of Reason, Commonweal,* L (1949): pp. 466–68.
Review of Bertrand de Jouvenel, *On Power, Commonweal,* L (1949): pp. 466–68.
"Agrarianism in Exile," *Sewanne Review*, LVIII (Autumn, 1950): pp. 586–606.
Review of Henry Steele Commager, *The American Mind, Commonweal,* LII (1950): pp. 101–103.
Review of Herbert Feis, *The Road to Pearl Harbor, Commonweal,* LII (1950): pp. 20–22.
Review of George Orwell, *Shooting an Elephant, Commonweal,* LIII (1950–51): pp. 283–84.
"Nehru: Philospher, Prophet, Politician," *Commonweal*, LIV (1951): pp. 432–33 (review of Jawaharlal Nehru and Norman Cousins, *Talks with Nehru*).
Review of Ferdinand A. Hermeus, *Europe Between Democracy and Anarchy, Commonweal,* LIV (1951): p. 266.
Review of Edward Crankshaw, *Cracks in the Kremlin Wall, Commonweal,* LIV (1951): p. 582.
"The Tennessee Agrarians," *Shenandoah,* III (1952): pp. 3–10.
"Aspects of the Southern Philosophy," *Hopkins Review*, V (1952): pp. 5–21 (reprinted in Louis D. Rubin, Jr., and Robert D. Jacobs, eds., *Southern Renascence* (Baltimore: John Hopkins University Press, 1953): pp. 14–30.
"Looking for an Agrument," *College English*, XIV (1952–53): pp. 210–16 (co-author).
"The Impact of Society on Mr. Russell," *Commonweal*, LVII (1953): p. 504 (review of Bertrand Russell, *The Impact of Science on Society*).
"And for Yale," *Commonweal*, LVIII (1953): pp. 31–32 (review of Editors of the *Yale Daily News, Seventy Five.*)

"Liberalism with a Ballast," *Sewanee Review*, LXII (April, 1954): pp. 334–41 (review of Lord Acton, *Essays on Church and State*; G.E. Fasnacht, *Acton's Political Philosophy;* and Gertrude Himmelfarb, *Lord Acton*).

Review of Russell Kirk, *A Program for Conservatives, Chicago Sunday Tribune Magazine of Books*, section IV (24 October 1954).

"History in a Dry Light," *Sewanne Review* LXIII (Spring, 1955): pp. 280–86 (review of Clement Eaton, *A History of the Southern Confederacy* and Thomas J. Pressley, *Americans Interpret Their Civil War*).

"Easy Conclusion," *National Review*, I (26 November 1955): p. 29 (review of Theodore L. Lentz, *Towards a Science of Peace*).

"The Best of Everything," *National Review,* I. (1 February 1956): pp. 21–22.

"The Middle of The Road: Where It Leads," *Human Events*, (24 March 1956).

"The Land and the Literature," *Sewanee Review*, LXIV (Summer, 1956): pp. 485–98 (review of Clifford Dowdey, *The Land They Fought For* and Willard Thorp, ed., *A Southern Reader*).

"Misunderstood Man," *National Review*, I (4 January 1956): p. 30 (review of Hudson Strode, *Jefferson Davis: American President*, 1808–1861).

"From Poetry to Bitter Fruit," *National Review*, I (8 February 1956): p. 26 (review of R. M. Hutchins, *The Great Books: The Foundation of a Liberal Education*).

"Language and the Crisis of Our Time," *National Review*, I (15 February 1956): p. 27 (review of I.A. Richards, *Speculative Instruments*).

"Cold Comfort," *National Review*, I (7 March 1956): p. 29 (review of R.M. MacIver, *The Pursuit of Happiness*).

"Flesh for a Skeleton," *National Review*, I (28 March 1956): p. 20 (review of Tobias Dantizig, *Number: The Language of Science*).

"Anybody's Guess," *National Review*, I (18 April 1956): p. 20 (review of P.M. Angle and E.S. Miers, eds., *The Living Lincoln*).

"On Social Science," *National Review*, I (9 May 1956): p. 20 (review of Stuart Chase, *The Proper Study of Mankind*).

"Safe for a While," *National Review*, II (20 June 1956): p. 21 (review of Lester Asheim, ed., *The Future of the Book*).

"Informed and Urbane," *National Review*, II (27 June 1956): p. 19 (review of John P. Dyer, *Ivory Towers in the Market Place*).

Review of S. F. Bemis, *John Quincy Adams and the Union, Freeman VI* (June, 1956): pp. 62–64.

"Which Ancestors?" *National Review*, II (25 July 1956): pp. 20–21 (review of Russell Kirk, *Beyond the Dreams of Avarice*).

"Inglorious Exit," *National Review*, II (18 August 1956): pp. 20–21 (review of Charles P. Smith, *James Wilson: Founding Father*).

"Social Science in Exceleis," *National Review*, II (26 September 1956): pp. 18–19 (review of Leonard White, ed., *The State of the Social Sciences*).

"Education for What?" *National Review*, II (24 November 1956): pp. 20–21 (review of J. D. Redden and F. A. Ryan, *A Catholic Philosophy of Education*).

Review of Arthur A. Ekrich, Jr., *The Decline of American Liberalism, Mississippi Valley Historical Review*, XLIII (1956–57): pp. 469–70.

"Person and Journalist," *National Review*, II (8 December 1956): p. 19 (review of Joseph F. Wall, *Henry Watterson, Reconstructed Rebel*).

"The South and the American Union," in Louis D. Rubin and James J. Kilpatrick, eds., *The Lasting South* (Chicago: Henry Regency Co., 1957): pp. 46–68.

"The Middle Way: A Political Meditation," *National Review, III* (20 January 1957): pp. 63–64.

"The Roots of Liberal Complacency," *National Review,* III (8 June 1957): pp. 541–43.

"Life Without Prejudice," *Modern Age,* I (Summer 1957): pp. 4–8.

"On Setting The Clock Right," *National Review,* IV (13 October 1957): pp. 321–23.

"Cotton Culture," *National Review,* III (16 March 1957): p. 264 (review of David L. Cohn, *The Life and Times of King Cotton*).

"The Western Star," *National Review,* III (13 April 1957): pp. 358–59 (review of Clement Eaton, *Henry Clay and the Art of American Politics*).

"Proud 'City of God,'" *National Review,* II (15 June 1957): p. 578 (review of Rene Guerdan, *Byzantium: Its Triumphs and Tragedy*).

"Integration is Communization," *National Review,* IV (13 July 1957): pp. 67–68 (review of Hugh D. Price, *The Negro and Southern Politics*; Carl T. Rowan, *Go South to Sorrow*; and Leo Kuper, *Passive Resistance in South Africa*).

Review of Amaury de Riencourt, *The Coming Caesars, Freeman,* VII (October, 1957): pp. 61–63.

"Trumpet-Toungued Foe of Coercion," *National Review,* IV (15 October 1957): pp. 307–308 (review of R.D. Meade, *Patrick Henry: Patriot in the Making*).

"Science and Sentimentalism," *National Review,* IV (7 December 1957): pp. 524–25 (review of Andre Missenard, *In Search of Man*).

"First in Peace," *National Review,* V (5 April 1958): pp. 329–30 (review of Douglas Southall Freeman, *George Washington: First in Peace*).

"The Lincoln-Douglas Debates," *National Review,* VI (21 June 1958): pp. 18–19 (review of P. M. Angle, ed., *Created Equal? The Complete Lincoln-Douglas Debates of 1858*).

"Open All the Way," *National Review,* VI (22 November 1958): pp. 339–40 (review of D. J. Boorstin, *The Americans: The Colonial Experience*).

Education and the Individual. Philadelphia: Intercollegiate Society of Individualists, 1959.

"Up From Liberalism," *Modern Age,* II (Winter, 1958–59): pp. 21–32.

"The Regime of the South," *National Review,* VI (14 March 1959): pp. 587–89.

"Concealed Rhetoric in Scientistic Sociology," *Georgia Review,* XIII (Spring, 1959): pp. 19–32.

"Contemporary Southern Literature," *Texas Quarterly,* II (Summer, 1959): pp. 126–44.

"Reconstruction: Unhealed Wound," *National Review,* VI (28 February 1959): pp. 559–60 (review of Hodding Carter, *The Angry Scar*).

Review of Forrest McDonald, *We The People, Freeman,* IX (May, 1959): pp. 58–62.

"Christian Letters," *Modern Age,* III (Fall, 1959): pp. 417–20 (review of Randall Stewart, *American Literature and Christian Doctrine*).

"Conservatism and Libertarianism: The Common Ground," *The Individualist,* IV (old series, May 1960): pp. 4–8.

"Mass Plutocracy," *National Review,* IX (5 November 1960): pp. 273–75, 290 (reprinted in *The Individualist,* V, October, 1960, pp. 5–8).

"Illusion of Illusions," *Modern Age,* IV (Summer, 1960): pp. 316–20 (review of M. Morton Auerbach, *The Conservative Illusion*).

"Dilemma of the Intellectual," *National Review,* IX (10 September 1960): pp. 153–54 (review of G. B. de Huszar, ed., *The Intellectual: A Controversial Portrait*).

Relativism and the Crisis of Our Time. Philadelphia: The Intercollegiate Society of Individualists. 1961.

"Reflections on Modernity," in *Speeches of the Year,* Brigham Young University, 1961.

"History or Special Pleading?" *National Review*, X (14 January 1961): pp. 21–22 (review of Harvey Wish, *The American Historian*).

"A Moral in a Word," *Modern Age*, V (Summer, 1961): pp. 330–31 (review of C. S. Lewis, *Studies in Words*).

"The Altered Stand," *National Review*, X (17 June 1961): pp. 389–90 (review of Robert Penn Warren, *The Legacy of the Civil War*).

"Modern Letters Con and Pro," *Modern Age*, V (Fall, 1961): pp. 426–27 (review of Edward Dahlberg and Sir Herbert Read, *Truth is More Sacred*).

"The Importance of Cultural Freedom," *Modern Age*, V (Winter, 1961–1962): pp. 21–34.

"A Hobble for Pegasus," *National Review*, XII (16 January 1962): pp. 30–31 (review of Robert E. Lane, *The Liberties of Wit*).

"A Great Individualist," *Modern Age*, VI (Spring, 1962): pp. 214–17 (review of Guy J. Forgue, ed., *Letters of H. L. Mencken*).

"Anatomy of Freedom," *National Review*, XIII (4 December 1962): pp. 443–44 (review of Frank S. Meyer, *In Defense of Freedom*).

Academic Freedom: The Principle and the Problems. Philadelphia: Intercollegiate Society of Individualists, 1963.

"Language is Sermonic," in R. E. Nebergall, ed., *Dimensions of Rhetorical Scholarship* (Norman, Oklahoma, 1963): pp. 49–63.

"Two Types of American Individualism," *Modern Age*, VII (Spring, 1963): pp. 119–34.

"The Southern Phoenix," *Georgia Review*, XVII (Spring, 1963): pp. 119–34.

"A Further Testament," *Modern Age*, VII (Spring, 1963): pp. 219–22 (review of Joseph Wood Krutch, *More Lives Than One*).

"The Image of Culture," from *Visions of Order*, reprinted in *Modern Age*, VIII (Spring, 1964): pp. 186–99.

"The Humanities in the Century of The Common Man," *New Individualist Review*, II, no. 3 (1964): pp. 17–24.

"The Southern Tradition," *New Individualist Review*, II, no. 3 (1964): pp. 7–16.

"Education and the Individual," reprinted in *Intercollegiate Review*, II (September, 1965): pp. 68–76.

"The American as a Regnerate Being," edited by George Core and M.E. Bradford, *Southern Review*, IV, n.s. (Summer, 1968): pp. 633–46.

"Realism and the Local Color Interlude," edited by George Core, *Georgia Review*, XXII (Fall, 1968): pp. 300–5.

"The Meaning of Name and Place," *Southern Partisan*, (Spring/Summer, 1991): pp. 15–16.

"The Pattern of a Life," *Southern Partisan*, (Fall, 1981): p. 13.

Essays and Articles on Richard M. Weaver

Amyx, Clifford. "Weaver the Liberal: A Memoir." *Modern Age*, (Spring, 1987): pp. 101–6.

Ancil, Ralph T. "Richard Weaver and the Metaphysics of Property." *Intercollegiate Review* (Spring, 1992): pp. 33–43.

Bliese, John. "Rhetoric and the Tyrannizing Image," *Modern Age* (Spring/Summer, 1984): pp. 208–14.

———"Richard M. Weaver, Russell Kirk and the Environment," *Modern Age* (Winter, 1996): pp. 148–158.

Bradford, M.E. "The Agrarianism of Richard Weaver: Beginnings and Completions," *Modern Age* (Summer/Fall, 1970): pp. 249–56.

——.(with George Core). Introduction to *The Southern Tradition at Bay.*

————Review of *Language is Sermonic*. In *National Review*. (17 November 1970).

Brown, Calvin S. "Southern Thought and National Materialism," *The Southern Literary Journal.* vol. I, no. II (Fall, 1969), review of *The Southern Tradition at Bay.*

Brownfeld, Allan. "The South Wisely Perceived," *University Bookman.* (Fall, 1989): pp. 17–22, review of *The Southern Essays of Richard Weaver.*

Core, George. "One View of The Castle: Richard Weaver and the Incarnate World of the South." In *The Poetry of Community: Essays on the Southern Sensibility of History and Literature*, edited by Lewis P. Simpson. Atlanta: Georgia State University, 1972.

———— Review of *Life Without Prejudice and Other Essays, Georgia Review*, (Fall 1967): p. 416.

————(with M.E. Bradford). Introduction to *The Southern Tradition At Bay.*

————Foreword to *The Southern Essays of Richard Weaver*, pp. xi-xiii.

Davidson, Donald. "The Vision of Richard Weaver." Foreword to *The Southern Tradition at Bay,* pp. 13–25.

———— "The Inspired Amatuer," *Modern Age* (Spring, 1966): pp. 206–7, review of *Life Without Prejudice and Other Essays.*

Davidson, Eugene. "Richard Malcolm Weaver—Conservative," *Modern Age* (Summer, 1963): pp. 226–30.

East, John P. "The Conservatism of Affirmation," *Modern Age* (Fall 1975): pp. 338–354 (also in *The American Conservative Movement: The Philosophical Founders.* Washington, D.C.: Regnery Gateway, 1986).

Ebbit, Wilma R. "Richard M. Weaver, Teacher of Rhetoric," *Georgia Review* (Winter 1963): pp. 415–18.

Eubanks, Ralph T. "Richard M. Weaver: In Memoriam," *Georgia Review* (Winter 1963): pp. 412–15.

Fermatt, John. Review of *Ideas Have Consequences, Catholic World* (June 1948): pp. 278–79.

Frankel, Charles. "Property, Language, and Piety," *The Nation* (29 May 1948): pp. 609–610, review of *Ideas Have Consequences.*

Garrison, W.E. "Unraveling Mr. Weaver," *The Christian Century,* (5 May 1948): pp. 415–16, review of *Ideas Have Consequences.*

Geiger, George R. "We Note...The Consequences of Some Ideas," *Antioch Review* (June 1948): pp. 251–54.

Havard, William C. "Richard Weaver: The Rhetor as Philosopher," in *The Vanderbilt Tradition: Essays in Honor of Thomas Daniel Young,* pp. 163–74. Baton Rouge: Louisiana State University Press, 1991.

Hobson, Fred. "Richard Weaver," in *Tell About the South: The Southern Rage To Explain,* pp. 323–335. Baton Rouge: Louisiana State University Press, 1983.

Johannesen, Richard L., Strickland, Rennard, and Eubanks, Ralph T. "Richard M. Weaver on the Nature of Rhetoric." Introduction to *Language is Sermonic*, pp. 7–30.

Jordan, Michael. "Richard Weaver and the True Southern Spirit," *Southern Partisan* (Spring 1988): pp. 34–36, review of *The Southern Essays of Richard Weaver.*

Kendall, Willmoore. "How to Read Richard Weaver: Philosopher of We The [Virtuous] People," *Intercollegiate Review* (September 1965): pp. 77–86.

———— Review of *Ideas Have Consequences,* in *Conservatism of Affirmation,* pp. 184–187. Chicago: Henry Regnery Company, 1963.

Kirk, Russell. "Ethical Labor," *Sewanee Review* (July 1954): pp. 485–503, review of *The Ethics of Rhetoric* and *The Quest For Community* by Robert Nisbet.

———— "Richard M. Weaver, R.I.P.," *National Review*, XIV (23 April, 1963): p. 308 (reprinted in *Confessions of a Bohemian Tory,* New York: Fleet Publishers, 1963 and *The Individualist,* September, 1963, 2).

———— Introduction to *Visions of Order.* Baton Rouge: Louisiana State Press, 1964.

Landess, Thomas. "Is The Battle Over…Or Has It Just Begun? The Southern Tradition Twenty Years After Richard Weaver." *Southern Partisan* (Spring, 1983): pp. 11–19.

Meyer, Frank S. "Richard M. Weaver: An Appreciation," *Modern Age* (Fall, 1970): pp. 243–48.

Milone, Victor, E. "The Uniqueness of Richard M. Weaver," *The Intercollegiate Review*, II (September, 1965): p. 67.

Montgomery, Marion. "Richard Weaver against the Establishment," in *The Men I Have Chosen For Fathers*, pp. 103–27. Columbia: University of Missouri Press, 1991.

Montgomery, Marion. "Richard M. Weaver, 1948," *Modern Age* (Summer/Fall 1982): pp. 252–255. Reprinted in a different form as "Afterword: Looking Before and After," in *The Men I Have Chosen For Fathers*, pp. 232–38. Columbia: University of Missouri Press, 1991.

Muller, Herbert J. "The Revival of the Absolute," *Antioch Review* (March, 1949): 99–110, review of *Ideas Have Consequences*.

Orton, W.A. Review of *Ideas Have Consequences, Commonweal* (14 May 1948): pp. 119–20.

Panchias, George A. "Irving Babbitt and Richard Weaver," *Modern Age* (Summer, 1996): pp. 267–76, review of *Visions of Order* and *Character and Culture: Essays on East and West* by Irving Babbitt.

Perry, Charner. Review of *Ideas Have Consequences*, *Ethics* (June, 1948): pp. 227–28.

Powell, James. "The Foundations of Weaver's Traditionalism," *New Individualist Review,* II, no. 3, (1964): pp. 3–6.

Regnery, Henry. "A Southern Agrarian at the University of Chicago," *Modern Age* (Spring, 1988): pp. 102–12.

Sullivan, Walter. "Richard Weaver and the Bishop's Widow," *Southern Literary Journal* (Spring, 1988). Reprinted in a different form in *In Praise of Blood Sports and Other Essays*, pp. 26–38. Baton Rouge: Louisiana State Press, 1990.

Talley, J.M. "The Last Fortress," *Modern Age* (Summer, 1964): pp. 305–7, review of *The Southern Tradition at Bay*.

Vivas, Eliseo. "Historian and Moralist," *Kenyon Review* (Spring, 1948): pp. 346–349, review of *Ideas Have Consequences* and *The Misinterpretation of Man* by Paul Roubiczek.

———— "The Mind of Richard Weaver," *Modern Age* (Summer, 1964): pp. 307–10, review of *Visions of Order*.

———— Introduction to *Life Without Prejudice and Other Essays.* Chicago: Henry Regnery, 1965.

Walraff, Charles F. Review of *The Ethics of Rhetoric, Arizona Quarterly* (Summer, 1954): pp. 183–85.

White, Bruce, A. "Dialectic Rhetorician," *Modern Age* (Summer/Fall, 1982): pp. 256–59.

Williamson, Jr., Chilton. "Stranger in Paradise," *National Review* (31 December 1985): pp. 96–98.

Index